SAILOR

SAILOR

PHILIP KAPLAN

PEN & SWORD
AVIATION

FOR MARGARET

First published in Great Britain in 2012 by
Pen & Sword Aviation
an imprint of
Pen & Sword Books Ltd
47 Church Street
Barnsley
South Yorkshire
S70 2AS

ISBN 000-0-00000-000-0

A CIP catalogue record for this book is
available from the British Library

Printed and bound in England
By CPI Group (UK) Ltd, Croydon, CR0 4YY

Pen & Sword Books Ltd incorporates the Imprints of Pen & Sword Aviation.
Pen & Sword Family History, Pen & Sword Maritime, Pen & Sword Military,
Pen & Sword Discovery, Wharncliffe Local History, Wharncliffe True Crime,
Wharncliffe Transport, Pen & Sword Select, Pen & Sword Military Classics,
Leo Cooper, The Praetorian Press, Remember When, Seaforth Publishing and
Frontline Publishing

For a complete list of Pen & Sword titles please contact
PEN & SWORD BOOKS LIMITED
47 Church Street, Barnsley, South Yorkshire, S70 2AS, England
E-mail: enquiries@pen-and-sword.co.uk
Website: www.pen-and-sword.co.uk

CONTENTS

SHOOTER 9

GENERAL BOTHA 16

A NEW YORK MINUTE 22

FLIGHT TRAINING 30

KIWI 36

SPITFIRE 43

HORNCHURCH 54

TEN COMMANDMENTS 70

FINGER-FOUR 76

KEEP UP WITH ME 85

BIGGIN HILL 97

COMBAT REPORT 106

FLYING SPRINGBOK 117

ON SCREEN 123

THE BLITZ 131

LEGEND 145

TORCH COMMANDO 155

REMEMBERING SAILOR 167

The author is particularly grateful to the following people for their kind, generous assistance in the research, preparation, and development of this book: Malcolm Bates, Geoff Barlow, Tony Bianchi, Kazmierz Budzik, Alan Deere, Bob Doe, Hugh Dundas, Royal Frey, Adolf Galland, James Goodson, Roger Hall, Eric Holloway, Charles Hewitt, Jack Ilfrey, Hargi and Neal Kaplan, Brian Kingcome, Walker Mahurin, Eric Marsden, Judy and Rick McCutcheon, Merle Olmsted, Geoffrey Page, Gunther Rall, Jeffrey Simmons, Peter Townsend, Hubert Zemke. Grateful acknowledgement to the following for the use of their text: David Bourne, D.S. Brookes, Stephen Bungay, Winston S. Churchill, Alan Deere, Len Deighton, Derek Dempster, Lovat Dickson, Sholto Douglas, Hugh Dowding, R.M.B. Duke-Woolley, John Freeborn, Wilfrid Gibson, Jonathan Glancey, Alex Henshaw, D.C. Inglis, Ira Jones, David Masters, May Morton, Edward R. Murrow, William Nasson, Cuthbert Orde, Keith Park, Ernie Pyle, Jeffrey Quill, Quentin Reynolds, W.M. Skinner, Henry Szczesny, Robert Stanford Tuck, Oliver Walker, John G. Winant, Derek Wood.

INTRODUCTION

"Upon this battle depends the survival of Christian civilisation. Upon it depends our own British life and the long continuity of our British institutions and our Empire. The whole fury and might of the enemy must very soon be turned on us now. Hitler knows that he will have to break us in this island or lose the war. If we can stand up to him, all Europe may be free and the life of the world may move forward into broad, sunlit uplands. But if we fail, then the whole world, including the United States, including all that we have known and cared for, will shrink into the abyss of a new Dark Age, made more sinister, and perhaps more protracted, by the lights of perverted science. Let us therefore brace ourselves to our duties, and so bear ourselves that, if the British Empire and its Commonwealth last for a thousand years, men will still say, 'This was their finest hour.' "
—Winston Churchill, House of Commons, 18th June 1940

Sailor Malan and his pilots pressed on with the fight in the daylight skies over southeast England, adding almost daily to the toll of enemy aircraft brought down, and to their own combat losses. Later that autumn, rains came; the Germans increased the pace of their bombing raids on London. The final phase of the Battle of Britain began.

"Taking a Spitfire into the sky in September 1940 was like entering a dark room with a madman waving a knife behind your back." — Sailor Malan

SHOOTER

At thirty he was too old for a fighter pilot, but he became the greatest of RAF fighter pilots. Adolph 'Sailor' Malan was not a gifted, instinctive pilot, but he became one. He was an exceptional shot, extraordinarily aggressive in air combat, a brilliant tactician, a great leader in the air, and a strict disciplinarian. Unlike many fighter pilots then and now, he was not a line-shooter or a big ego.

He devised ten commandments, his rules for air fighting, which guided and saved the lives of countless British and American fighter pilots in the Second World War and since. He had good, basic values and cared about the men in his command. He spent extra time with the newest and least experienced of them, showing them the ropes and doing all he could to keep them from making the kinds of mistakes that might get them killed.

The community of Wellington sits on the bank of the Kromme River in South Africa's Western Cape, a 45-minute drive from Cape Town. Local tourism people tout its virtues in agriculture, wine and brandy-making, and point out the thrilling experience one can have on a game drive through the heart of the Cape Winelands, observing white-tailed wildebeest, springbuck, grey rhebuck and other exotic species. They call attention to the town's position as an academic centre and refer to Huguenot College as a shining example of its educational heritage.

French Huguenots had come to the area in 1694 during the reign of King Louis XIV, when religious persecution caused them to flee France for a new start in South Africa. The transplanted Huguenots shared the developing area with many Dutch settlers, starting farms in the pleasant Val du Charron, which became known as Valley of the Wagonmakers, and was the early focus of the Wellington community. Jacques Malan was the first of his family to settle on that fertile land.

The Huguenots were hard-working, practical planters, well grounded in tending, pruning and watering. Most of them, including Malan, thrived and prospered, as did their numerous descendants. One of them was Willem Malan, Willie to all who knew him in the valley. Evelyn, his wife, gave birth to their son, Adolph Gysbert, on October 3rd 1910, and the boy spent much of his early life at Slent, the family farm in the Cape. It was a time and place he always recalled fondly: "The soul of South Africa lies there. The whole landscape is a painter's dream, for between these enormous buttresses sustaining the southernmost end of South Africa's inland plateau, are the valleys in which the first Huguenot families settled in the 1690s when the Cape settlement itself was only forty years old. I love my country and I am longing to get back there with my wife and children. It is a wonderful country for children to grow up in." The old farmstead was ideally set on the green slopes of the Paardeberg or Horse Mountain, sixteen miles south of Adolph's Wellington birthplace. The area was lush with great oaks, vineyards and fruit trees, and the spectacular Table Mountain was visible twenty miles to the south.

Throughout his boyhood Adolph was intrigued by guns and firearms, an interest encouraged by his father who, on one particular Sunday afternoon when the boy was eight years old, called him into the house and handed him a double-barrelled shotgun. Giving him a handful of cartridges, Willie said: "Go and shoot something for the pot." Sailor remembered: "I suppose he was joking. I was small for my age, but my father seemed to like thrusting responsibility onto me, and he must have had a purpose in doing so.

"I went outside and scored a bull's eye on a watering can.

That got me into trouble later. Then I tried creeping up behind a turtle-dove. How I was able to get the gun to my shoulder and fire, I don't know, but I did. Unfortunately, I fired off both barrels at once and the recoil knocked me flat and bruised my shoulder for days after. When I reloaded the gun I got the rim of one of the cartridges jammed in the breech. I struggled very hard to break the gun open, but I hadn't the strength. In the end I took it back under my arm, and ran into the lounge to my mother, still wrestling with the triggers and pointing the barrels towards her. She was terribly angry, and snatched the gun from me. I was scolded and so was my father for letting me have the gun. I wasn't allowed to handle a shotgun for a long time after that."

Two conflicts known to history as the Boer (farmer descendants of the Dutch settlers) Wars were fought in the latter part of the nineteenth century between the British and the independent Boer republics, Transvaal and the Orange Free State. The first of these, the Transvaal War of 1880-81, occurred when the Boers rebelled against British rule in the Transvaal. Then in 1899, the "rooibaatjes" or redcoat troops from several British possessions battled the Boers resulting in the conversion of the Boer republics into British colonies, which later became the Union of South Africa. This war lasted until 1902 and divided the loyalties of the various Malans. Willie's brother Piet favoured the Boers, while Willie supported the British cause.

In the second Boer War, General Jan Christiaan Smuts led commandos against the British in attacks on their vital supply lines in the Highveld region. In one of these raids, at Twenty-four Rivers, Willie Malan was astride his horse when struck by rifle fire from one of Smuts' men. The first bullet ripped through both of his thighs, shattering one of the bones. The second round opened a massive wound on his right arm. As he lay in the Wellington hospital the leg began to supperate and the medical staff debated whether to amputate. In the end Willie kept the leg, but for the next six years, he struggled around on crutches, a virtual invalid. Ultimately, he lost patience with the doctors and set about trying to cure himself of the nearly constant pain and discomfort. Eventually, he was able to ride again and do limited work on the family farm.

Growing up at Slent was a storybook adventure for Adolph and his younger brother, Ralph. Baboons still sheltered in the rocky upper reaches of the farm and, in times when food was scarce, the animals frequently came down to raid the big fig tree behind the farmhouse. The family dogs then chased the baboons who in turn chased the dogs. While amusing, this never matched the thrill the boys had in boar baiting. They were captivated by teasing a great grey beast with savage tusks and a vicious attitude, and for the rest of his life Sailor carried a scar on his arm from a close encounter in a Boar War of his own: "When I exploded a clod of earth right on his snout, that boar had made up his mind to get me. Once you get a pig's mind set in one direction you never shake him off. He must have chased Ralph and me more than a mile through the orchards and out onto the mountainside before he finally caught up with me. I was winded, and so was he, but he had some steam to spare. I could feel him closing in and just managed to jump and catch hold of the branch of a tree. Unfortunately the branch broke, and I fell on his back. He carried me a couple of yards, and then, when I dropped, he swung round and tried to savage me. And that's when I got this . . ."

The new European settlers had been viewed with curiosity by their nine million native African and Bantu tribe neighbours. The matter of language soon led to a conflict and many a feud in the region. The Huguenots found that their own language was being overwhelmed by Dutch. This was followed some generations later, when the Cape became an English possession, by the order that only English be spoken. Gradually, a tug-of-war developed between the champions of three languages for the region: High Dutch—the language and written medium of the church; English—the tongue of officialdom, the schools and high society; and Afrikaans— used by the farmers and frontiersmen.

By the time of the Act of Union in 1910, Dutch and English had become the two official languages, until 1925 when a Parliamentary committee decided Afrikaans was preferable to Dutch. Since then, proponents of both English and Afrikaans have vied for communicating supremacy, a powerful example being the determined effort by Dr Daniel Malan, a distant cousin, but a polar opposite to Sailor in most respects, to develop a racial bloc of Afrikaans-speaking South Africans. Sailor recalled though, that Bilingualism in his district was such that a man would often start a sentence in Afrikaans and finish in English. At home his family generally spoke English. His mother was English-born and his father spoke English well. His parents' plan was that, although they were bilingual, they felt it was better to speak one language well rather than have their rapidly growing family talking a mixture of the two.

There were a few farm schools in the neighbourhood, each with about fifteen or twenty children from local farms. That was Adolph's first schooling before attending Stellenbosch, and it took him to the Standard IV level. He never forgot one teacher, Miss M. from the Transvaal. She was still very bitter about the British Tommies in the Boer War. What she had to say about them—and the English generally, didn't make sense to Adolph. He knew all of his mother's English family, and played with her brothers Clifford and Edwin. Miss M.

wanted the children to believe that the *rooibaatjes* not only behaved like devils, but looked something like them—all pock-marked, with red necks and purple morals. It left a nasty impression on Adolph, all that hatred. He had thought she may have had some family reason for being so fanatical. But it didn't work on him the way she obviously wished it to.

Adolph had another shock when he started at the Stellenbosch school in Standard V. He discovered a sort of linguistic segregation being practised in the classrooms— English-speaking on the one side, Afrikaans-speaking on the other. He recalled it making a very bad impact on his young mind. He had friends on both sides of the class and among themselves there was no question of language dividing them. They spoke English or Afrikaans impartially. In the farm school Miss M. had taught them in Afrikaans, but the school books were all in English. It seemed to him to be the easiest and the most natural thing in the world to switch from one to the other.

After the end of the First World War, the crippled Willie Malan finally had to face the fact that operating the farm at Slent was beyond his capability. As a business, it was not prospering and he decided to get rid of many of his older vines in order to plant orchards of plums, peaches and apricots. But a serious economic decline followed in the wake of the war, and he was forced to sell Slent at a considerable loss and move the family, first to Stellenbosch and then back to Wellington. There, Adolph went to the Boy's High School, where the motto was *Mikhoog*, or Aim High. To help with the family finances, his mother took in boarders and did dressmaking. She noticed that Adolph was more and more independent and, six months after his thirteenth birthday, he told his parents that he wanted to become a cadet in the merchant navy aboard the training ship *General Botha*, a vessel which was left at permanent anchor off Simonstown on False Bay, across the peninsula from Cape Town. He had made up his mind to go to sea even though he knew that he was still underage and academically deficient for acceptance. Many years later, his mother commented on an article in an American magazine which stated that Sailor had a photo of the Royal Navy ship H.M.S. *Hood* pinned on his bedroom wall during his high school days and the picture had inspired him to be a sailor: "I'm sorry. It's a nice story, but I've no recollection of it. Certainly not in his Wellington days before he joined the ship. We were living in Malherbe Street then and Adolph and Ralph slept on the stoop. I had boarders in the other bedrooms. I don't think I would have forgotten if there had been such a picture on the wall."

GENERAL BOTHA

When the historian and author Oliver Walker interviewed Sailor Malan in the early 1950s, Walker was moved by the effect on Malan of his 1924 experience as a cadet aboard the South African training ship *General Botha*. Walker: "In talks with Sailor during which he described incidents infinitely more dramatic and perilous than anything that happened aboard the *Botha*, I never saw him more emotionally stirred than when he recalled the ceremony of being tied down and thrashed. The memory of it had stayed with him vividly as a deed of outrage, an invasion of pride and privacy that helped to fashion a kind of stoicism that became an armour-plating for more strenuous days to come. Its immediate effect was to check in him any desire, when he in turn became an Old Salt, to take advantage of his seniority, and it had much to do with his reluctance, in later years, to join in the horseplay of RAF squadron initiatory customs."

It was the death of South African cadet Howard Davis in Flanders during the first year of World War One that moved his father, T.B.F. Davis, a wealthy former master mariner from Durban, to memorialize his son through the purchase of the elderly British cruiser H.M.S. *Thames* in 1921. Young Davis had been a cadet in H.M.S. *Worcester* and his father wanted to make a gift of a cruiser to his nation for the training of its future merchant seamen. The *Thames* had been scheduled for its final voyage, a one-way trip to the knacker's yard. It had been judged "too weak to fight and too slow to run away". Davis, however, thought it ideal for his purposes and sent it to be fully renovated before presenting it to his government, which chose to rename it *General Botha*, honouring the memory of the Union of South Africa's first Prime Minister, Louis Botha. The ship was to serve as a moored training vessel for, on average, 120 boys between the ages of fourteen and sixteen, roughly half of whom were English-speaking and the other half Dutch or Afrikaans-speaking. Luckily for the underage and academically underqualified Adolph, those in charge of the ship's administration were interpreting their own rules somewhat loosely when he applied to be a cadet. The administrators were having trouble filling their own quota of Afrikaans-speaking trainees and, as Malan qualified in that sense, was personable, good-looking and healthy, they bent the rules a bit and accepted him.

The captain and some of the instructors in *Botha* were charged with creating a "Botha Boy" tradition virtually overnight, a vision of the ideal trainee fashioned after those of the British merchant navy training vessels H.M.S. *Conway*, *Pangbourne*, and *Worcester*. A simple glass case aboard the *Botha* displayed her only link to any sort of tradition—a small fragment of Admiral Nelson's H.M.S. *Victory* mounted above the inscription "Forever England." Those in charge of *Botha* knew that turning their trainees into effective, responsible, successful merchant seamen, in line with the new Botha Boy tradition, believed that that goal could only be achieved through stern discipline and the tightest adherence to ship's rules.

The shipboard routine began each day with reveille at 5:45 a.m. followed by showers, cleaning, the stowing of hammocks and other kit, a meagre breakfast, and a long, hard day of work and study under constant supervision. The boys were required to wash their own clothes and their dishes after meals, to scrub the decks and keep the ship ship-shape. The term lasted from February through December and was broken only by a weekend liberty once each month, for the boys to have a bit of shore time.

The Botha Boys were expected to make their way through

a two-year curriculum that emphasized seamanship. The subject matter focused on navigation with logs, chart work, Mercator's and plane sailings, meteorology, latitude by meridian altitude, longitude by chronometer, gunnery, signalling, drill, and considerable boat handling and the manning of skiffs and cutters between the ship and shore. Adolph was particularly interested in the gunnery instruction, which included pistol and rifle firing, the stripping and mounting of guns, sight setting, tracing gun circuits, and the understanding of explosives.

From his first day aboard, he was exposed to two distinct forms of regulation: institutionalized bullying and ship's discipline. In the first instance, a clique of senior second-year cadets known as "the terrible three" exerted their dominance over the sixty new boys with whom Adolph had arrived. Through a combination of bullying, extortion and a protection racket, the three gangsters-in-training, at least one of whom would later end up in prison, sought control over the new cadets. One of their favourite ploys was to show the neophytes how to sling a hammock. They used a slip-knot so that one of them could come round after lights out, target a cadet who had just struggled into his awkward, swinging nightnet, and give the slip-knot a hefty jerk, sending the hapless lad sprawling on the deck. These same "Old Salts" revelled in making the new boys run a gauntlet of lashes from what were known as "rope ends," a short piece of heavy rope wielded like a small club or blackjack.

The rope-end punishment was a practise of the ship's instructors, a part of the basic discipline, which had been copied by the upperclassmen. One of Adolph's instructors remarked that discipline was discipline, and no arguments. A rope's end now and again did them more good than any soft soap or motherly love. If we saw any cadet not doing exactly the right thing we found that the nearest rope's end had a more direct effect than all the words of advice. One or two cracks administered and taken in the true spirit worked wonders. The gunnery instructor used to come to the hammock of a cadet who had irritated him during the day and would order the boy to climb down, bend over, touch his toes, and 'take his medicine like a man.' Of the gauntlet, Sailor remembered: "I can still feel the lashes after a lapse of twenty-eight years."

One offence that always attracted punishment was violating the no smoking rule, which was strictly enforced due to the particular fire hazard aboard the *Botha*. Boys being what they are, the cadets took whatever clandestine opportunities that arose to sneak a puff, even though the penalty if caught was six cuts of a cane. The master-at-arms had a strong arm and six strokes from him were enough to curb anybody for a time. They used to be given in the recreation room where, on the floor by the table, were two ring-bolts. Through these a rope could be passed which bound one down on the table. One had to be certified as fit to take his medicine. This was the sick bay steward's job. He would hang on to one end of the rope, holding one down while the boy was being thrashed. One was only allowed to wear No 1 duck trousers to receive this punishment. These were shorts which became very tight when one stretched over. 'Cadet So-and-so is now ready for his punishment, sir,' the NCO would report to the master-at-arms, who would then select a cane— he usually gave himself a choice of two or three—and step forward. When he stepped forward one bit harder on the squeegee, a piece of rubber one kept in the mouth to stop yourself yelling. With six cuts it was easy to draw blood, after which one couldn't sit down in comfort for a week.

Adolph: "The first time I saw this punishment handed out was to a big chap—an Old Salt. It was quite a shock to see him break down. Later on I understood why." Adolph got his share of discipline while aboard the *Botha*, and it may be that the instructor who thought it did the boys more good than motherly love was right. It certainly made a deep and lasting impression on him.

In the course of Adolph's second term aboard the *Botha*, the Royal Navy battleship H.M.S. *Repulse* sailed into the bay and anchored near the training vessel. A special guest aboard the battleship was the then Prince of Wales, the present Duke of Windsor, who was touring the Union. During the two-month visit of the *Repulse*, teams of boys from *Botha* challenged and beat cadets from the battleship in cricket, boxing, rowing, and soccer. Both sides greatly enjoyed the contests and the South Africans felt privileged to tour the great warship, inspect its massive guns and sense the power it projected.

While well-liked, enthusiastic, and a hard worker, Adolph was never more than average scholastically. His weakest area was mathematics, an essential ingredient in the educational mix of one who wanted to sail as an officer in his country's merchant fleet. That shortcoming, together with his still being underage in 1926 at the end of his term in the *Botha*, meant he would be spending a further six months aboard the vessel before finally passing the course with a good record and a First Extra certificate in seamanship. It was Adolph's driving urge then to get to sea. For some time he had had an odd feeling that everything depended on him. He felt cut off—on his own, as if he'd burnt his boats behind him—the ones ashore. He could never think of returning home, or of going home to stay. He was trained for the sea, and that was the home he wanted. He knew it wasn't an easy time for his parents. He thought too, that by going away, being completely independent, he would be saving them some anxiety, financial and otherwise. His was a very big family by then—two sisters and four brothers—the youngest, Peter, only a baby, and all of them younger than him. Slent had been sold at a bad loss. His father's health was poor. When Willie was well enough to think of working he was offered the manager-ship of a fruit farm at Riverside in the Golden Valley Citrus Estates. That happened before Adolph went to sea. So there was a complete uprooting of the family from all the old scenes. He knew how difficult it was for them. For himself, by that time, he could focus on only one thing—getting away to sea."

On May 14th, 1947, many years after Adolph Malan had left the *General Botha* for the final time, the old training ship again bore her original name, H.M.S. *Thames*. It was her last day afloat. The Scala gun battery on a hill above Simonstown began firing a succession of twenty-four heavy shells into her hull, but the eighty-one year old former Royal Navy cruiser resisted being sunk. Then, as the fifth shell slammed into her amidships, she shuddered. Several fires erupted on her main deck and below decks, sending a pall of thick black smoke out low over the sea nine miles off Roman Rock Lighthouse and she slowly began a list to port. A small party of Admiralty observers stood nearby on a tug watching as the list grew more extreme. Naval personnel had placed an array of explo-sive charges aboard the *Botha* against the possibility that the Scala shelling might fail to sink the old ship. They watched for several minutes as the big shells impacted the hull of *Botha*, considering whether to detonate the charges. Slowly the cruiser extended her list until the masts were nearly par-allel to the water. The sea crept over her stern, her bow rose, and the old hulk paused and slipped beneath the surface.

A NEW YORK MINUTE

Young Adolph Malan secured his first post-cadet position, and eight months after graduating from his course on the *General Botha* training vessel, he boarded the Union-Castle Steamship Line's *Sandown Castle* at Port Elizabeth harbour. With her general cargo loading completed, the *Sandown Castle* sailed for New York. It was 1927 and another young adventurer was about to cross the Atlantic, in the opposite direction.

The aviator Charles Lindbergh, later known as "The Lone Eagle"and "Lucky Lindy", was determined to make the first solo non-stop flight across the Atlantic ocean. In 1919, Raymond Ortieg, a New York City hotel owner, had put up a prize of $25,000 for the first person to fly non-stop from New York to Paris. Several pilots had been killed trying for the Orteig prize, but Lindbergh felt he could win it if he had the right aeroplane. With the financial assistance of several St. Louis businessmen, Lindbergh asked Ryan Aeronautical Company of San Diego to design and build that special plane which he named the *Spirit of St. Louis*.

He took off from Roosevelt Field, New York, at 7:52 a.m. on May 20th, 1927 and landed at Le Bourget airfield, Paris, thirty-three and one-half hours later to the cheers of thousands of people gathered for his arrival. U.S. President Calvin Coolidge awarded him the Congressional Medal of Honor and the Distinguished Flying Cross. Lindbergh: "The life of an aviator seemed to me ideal. It involved skill. It brought adventure. It made use of the latest developments of science. Mechanical engineers were fettered to factories and drafting boards while pilots have the freedom of wind with the expanse of sky. There were times in an aeroplane when it seemed I had escaped mortality to look down on earth like a God."

Like so many people in that time, Adolph Malan was dazzled by Lindbergh's achievement. The American aviator was a heroic figure to the young South African seaman whose second voyage arrival in New York coincided with the immense Wall Street ticker-tape parade in which more than four million Americans cheered Lindbergh. It was the most spectacular event of its kind since the end of the Great War. To Malan, Lindbergh's life exemplified the adventurous, high-achieving sort that he wanted for himself and, while he had never before had any real interest in aviation or flying, the Lindbergh flight had stirred something in him that he could not ignore.

During the next nine years aboard the ships of the Union Castle Line, he visited New York and Philadelphia many times and was always powerfully impressed by the enthusiastic, hard-driving American spirit and the apparent wealth of opportunity there. New York was in some ways like a second home to him and he never failed to be excited by the first glimpse of its unique skyline as his ship entered the harbour.

The lifestyle of a young merchant seaman in foreign ports has always been packed with a range of temptations, some of them best given a wide berth. Common sense, restricted financial resources, and the presence and influences of the British Apprentice Club, helped steer him clear of most such threats.

The club was located in an annexe of the Hotel Chelsea at 222 West 23rd Street, between Seventh and Eighth Avenues. Since its opening in 1883, the hotel's magnetic attraction has drawn the famous and the notorious from the worlds of art, science, letters, music, and the stage, including Eugene O'Neill, Thomas Wolfe, Arthur Miller, Arthur C. Clarke, Dylan Thomas, Janis Joplin, Jimi Hendrix, Jasper Johns, Willem de Kooning, Tennessee Williams, Mark Twain, Simone de Beauvoir, Jean-Paul Sartre, Robert Oppenheimer, Lillie Langtry, Edith Piaf, Andy Warhol and many more.

British merchant ships have always tended to remain in the port of New York for relatively long periods, affording their crews ample time in the city where most of them had no connections and few if any friends. For thousands of lonely young merchant sailors, the British Apprentice Club has provided a warm and welcoming haven in Manhattan.

In 1921 two American women, Katherine Mayo and Moyca Newell, wanted to do something to reciprocate for the hospitality the British had shown American soldiers during the war in 1917-18. They decided to found the club in the city.

The British Apprentice Club was intended to be a cozy, home-like "fireside corner", always open, with no rules. It was to be for cadet seamen between the ages of sixteen and twenty. There they could meet new friends, especially young American girls 'from good homes', play games, write letters, dance, and share the company of 'an American mother figure' with whom they could confide their deepest feelings, someone to quell the concerns of their own far away mothers. Staffed with young, attractive hostesses, the club proved a pleasant and ideal home away from home for Adolph and many of his mates. He soon became a regular visitor there and was well remembered by one of the hostesses who recalled him as being very blond with a young, almost girlish face and a shy, diffident manner.

"When introductions were taking place, Adolph was usually hidden behind a group of other boys, and was sometimes overlooked altogether. Invariably, he was the last to be introduced, but often made the greatest impression. He was always immaculately groomed and very fastidious— always wore the correct tie, hat, and shoes to match the suit he wore. He noticed well-dressed women, too. He had a pleasing, soft, educated voice and disliked intensely loud raucous voices or crude behaviour in other people. He was very sensitive to his surroundings and associations.

"He worried a great deal about passing his examinations. At the time, no one thought that he was spectacular as far as intellectual pursuits were concerned—he was not interested in literature of any kind. But he had keen powers of observation and was a serious thinker. He loved to take part in serious discussions. That, it seemed, was how he obtained most of his information. He derived great pleasure in conversing with mature people. One lady in particular was a great friend of his and she gave him a great deal of advice and understanding in his most bewildered moments, of which he had many. His first thought when he arrived in New York was usually to get in touch with her.

"Adolph was sympathetic and thoughtful of others, idealistic, and somewhat introspective. He was forever trying to analyse his emotions and his actions. It distressed him more than average if he didn't always do the right thing. He lacked self-confidence. He once wrote in a letter "My whole life is a succession of minor indecisions and therefore I compromise by more or less drifting along and snatching at what happiness I can find along the way." His friends thought he probably realized later that this was just inex-perienced youth, and that experience gives assurance, but whereas most young people think they know everything, he was always doubtful of his abilities.

"He was quite a social lion and received many invitations to parties at which he was always a great asset, as he was quite popular. He liked to have a drink occasionally for sociability, but never to excess. He would never make an exhibition of himself and was always restrained in his behaviour—always perfectly controlled—in fact this was so in all matters. He never seemed excited over anything except his training in the Royal Navy, and he could talk on the subject of gunnery and give one a complete lecture on the operations.

"He was most courteous and friendly to everyone, and patient; never irritable. He loved to dance and was always available; he never sat out dances while there was some girl without a partner, though he was only an average dancer and stuck to his own routine which never varied. He always offered to take some girl home from all dances without fuss and discrimination, provided his own particular friends were not present, or were otherwise taken care of. He was very reliable and seldom promised anything he could not carry out.

"His biggest problem in those early years was how his future would turn out. He knew he did not want to go to sea all his life, because, as he remarked, 'it was a constant round of making friends and saying good-bye.' A sailor's life was too uncertain for him—he wanted a more settled existence— a home and family (six children was one of his dreams). But he couldn't decide just what he should strive for. When the Air Force was suggested to him, he was positive he would not like to fly. None of his friends were sure what caused him to change his mind. That happened in England. He did once say that he would like to enter politics—in South Africa.

"He had a retentive memory. For example, the last time he was in New York as a sailor he received a torn dollar bill which he was afraid had no value. A friend volunteered to find out if it was usable and gave him a good one in its place. It turned out to be quite good and the friend immediately forgot about it. In 1941 (seven years later) when he paid the U.S. a visit during the war, he pulled out of his pocket a new dollar bill to replace the one he was quite sure had been valueless."

In his nine years with the Union Castle Line, Adolph served aboard nine different ships. In his voyages to New

York throughout the late 1920s and early 1930s, he witnessed many changes, not least being the era of Prohibition. Malan: 'You could go into any corner drug store and see a cop getting his 'tot'. I didn't touch the stuff much myself. We were warned off it. But even kids were roped into the bootlegging racket. The change came in 1929, after the Wall Street crash. It seemed to me that the whole nation took a knock then. Before, they were cheerful, very hospitable, arrogant, on top of the world. After the fall they appeared stunned, rather frightened.'

With the great depression unemployment soared in much of the world. The Union Castle Line was forced to temporarily end its employment of apprentice seamen, but it continued to look after its young officers. In that harsh period, Adolph sat the exam for his second mate certificate. He was not laid off, but the only work the company could keep him in was as a watchman of idle cargo in the Southampton docks, with the occasional trip across the North Sea to Hamburg in a small coaster. Malan: 'I'd say it bred in me a kind of fatalism. Long voyages get you into a certain frame of mind. You're signed on. You know your destination weeks ahead. In the meantime you jog along in a routine which seldom varies. You get, too, a feeling of not belonging anywhere in particular.' "

Lynda Fraser, the girl he would marry, was sixteen when Adolph was introduced to her by mutual friends in London in 1930. He impressed her as very serious and rather inarticulate. They would not meet again until three years later. On his occasional visits to South Africa in the '30s, he saw his family at their home in Riverside, Golden Valley, and they found him to have filled out nicely and developed into a well-muscled young man. They noted his strong American accent and the pipe that now was his constant companion.

As the decade wore on conversation seemed invariably to

turn to the possibility, and then the liklihood, of war in Europe. On his trips to Germany, Adolph was keenly aware of an aggressive spirit there and a growing perception of some kind of new destiny. "I spent a lot of time talking to German harbour officials, sailors, and civilians, and their attitude made me realize that war was inevitable." By 1935, he had sailed to the United States for the last time as an officer of the Merchant Navy. He was third officer aboard his old ship, the *Sandown Castle*. Following that trip he sat the exam for his first mate's certificate and completed a six-week training course with the Royal Naval Reserve at Devonport, which would prove useful in the coming conflict. "It was a first class intensive course. You learnt odd things like how to make allowance for heating in cordite when live shells were used. Our final tests were at sea when we were given ten salvoes to play with and had to hit a moving target being towed anything from between five and ten miles away and at high speed. I managed to straddle the target four or five times which gave me a good number of extra high marks." The R.N.R. training concluded with a period of manoeuvres in H.M.S. *Malaya*, a *Queen Elizabeth*-class battleship which had taken part in the Battle of Jutland in 1916.

With his recent training, and nine years of service with the steamship line behind him, Adolph now gave increasing thought to his future in light of the incessant talk of war and his impatience with the notion of a continuing life at sea. He decided to apply for a Short Service Commission in the General Duties branch of the Royal Air Force and, thanks in part to a glowing recommendation by the management of the training ship *General Botha*, he was accepted. "I enjoyed myself in the Navy and wouldn't have missed it, but I found it starch-ridden. I didn't like the caste system. I can see its attractions and its value. Within its limits it produces, more often than not, an efficient class of officer. But it didn't suit me, either by temperament or by comparison with the life I'd known in the merchant service. The attitude of regular Naval types to RNR, and RNVR, was as if we were the lowest form of life. The biggest mistake, as I saw it from an outsider's viewpoint, was the lack of human relations. The men lived, as it were, below stairs, and the officers only addressed them and knew them as underlings. The difference in relationships when I joined the RAF, was remarkable."

FLIGHT TRAINING

The original Bristol Filton Flying Ground opened 100 years ago, near the Bristol and Colonial Aeroplane Company works atop Filton Hill, north of the city. Histories of the aerodrome briefly mention that a flying school was once located on the northern side of the airfield, where the engine division of the aeroplane company was situated until the 1980s, when it was bulldozed to make way for a new Post Office sorting centre.

Adolph Malan arrived at the Bristol Aeroplane Company Flying School, in early January 1936. He and his fellow pupil pilots were told that in seven weeks, if they successfully completed their course, they would be appointed Acting Pilot Officers and would be sent on to advanced pilot training at No 3 Flying Training School, Grantham in Lincolnshire. His class of thirteen students included three who had been chosen from the air force ranks for training to be sergeant pilots. Adolph was the oldest in the class and, by virtue of his naval training and service, the most experienced.

The actual flying part of the course was conducted in the De Havilland Tiger Moth trainer and amounted to twenty-five hours of dual instruction and twenty-five hours solo flying. Adolph was among the first students to solo and on completion of the course was rated "above average." Before that, however, in the early days of his flying, he was somewhat disillusioned. He was bemused by the sight of the other students, who seemed to take quite naturally to the business of flight, making perfect turns and flawless landings, while he struggled with the unfamiliar aeroplane and environment.

The students were accommodated in the tiny, uncomfortable quarters of a converted wooden hut near the field. Worrying about his competence on the course, he began to doubt the wisdom of joining the air force and wondered if he might have burnt his naval bridges prematurely. The chances of mastering the Tiger Moth, or even developing sufficient skill to be able to solo in the machine, seemed remote. Then, "Suddenly, I got a few landings right and Deacon, the instructor, an ex-fighter pilot from Royal Flying Corps days, smiled and said 'Off you go.' " Adolph finished the course at Filton, but not without his instructor noting in his final report: "This pilot is inclined to be heavy and impatient at the controls."

The Royal Air Force grew out of the Royal Flying Corps of the First World War, whose Marshal, 'Boom' Trenchard, had built it into an enormous organisation of 30,000 officers, 260,000 men and 35,000 aircraft by October 1918, when the war was nearing an end. Britain's new air force had considerable appeal to independent young men like Adolph, an appeal that far outshone that of the army. Starting with the uniform itself, the airmen had no need for riding boots, field boots or puttees. Also gone were the swagger sticks and swords for the officers. Structurally, the RAF set out to create a network with solid sources for its various personnel requirements. A Volunteer Reserve was established which combed the public schools for appropriate senior student candidates, and training schools for apprentices were started at Halton and Cosford. A programme of expansion for the civilian flying schools was put in place and a range of specialist schools was created for navigators, wireless operators, observers, and gunners. Such was the level of interest and enthusiasm in aviation among British young men that flying was seriously challenging traditional sport for weekend activity.

Adolph and his fellow Acting Pilot Officers from the Filton class moved on to advanced training at No 3 Flying Training School, Grantham, where they learned to fly Hawker Hinds and Audaxes in 100 flight hours over a period of nine months which was broken into two terms. Between graduating from the Filton course and reporting to Grantham, the officer trainees were posted to RAF Uxbridge for two weeks, primarily to allow them time in London to have tailors outfit them with their air force uniforms. At Uxbridge they were also instructed in Mess Rules, drill and etiquette. In his brief free time, Adolph managed to squeeze in a quick trip to see Lynda, his girl friend, in Ruislip, near London.

Once again, Adolph's age, experience and charm worked in his favour on arrival at No 3 FTS, where he was made Course Commander, a position he would retain throughout his time at the Grantham base. There he was immediately given the nickname "Admiral" because of his naval background.

Wing Commander Roland Robert Stanford Tuck DSO, DFC & Two Bars, AFC, learned to fly on that course at No 3 FTS with Malan. Tuck was credited with twenty-seven aerial kills, two shared destroyed, and six probables in his impressive wartime career. Shot down on January 28th, 1942, during a low-level fighter sweep over northern France, he was forced to crash-land his badly damaged Spitfire. Captured by German troops, he spent the next two years as a prisoner of war in Stalag Luft III, Sagan. He successfully escaped on February 1st, 1945, while the camp was being evacuated ahead of approaching Russian forces. After the war he flew as a test pilot on the Canberra programme for English Electric before settling into his ultimate career as a mushroom farmer in Kent.

Tuck did his flying training at Grantham in the company of his friend 'Sailor' Malan. Tuck thought Sailor was one of the greatest fighter leaders of the war. From their training days they shared the view that if one was not flying accurately, it was no good pushing the firing button and hoping for the best. If one opened fire with the bank and turn indicator showing a bad skid either way, the bullets would go nowhere near where you thought you were aiming as you looked through the graticule of the gunsight.

They had a certain kinship, both having been cadets in the Merchant Service. He remembered Malan being a very good looking, solid, square shouldered, blonde chap, and how they were kept very busy over nearly a year's intensive training with ground studies, meteorology, air navigation, engines, rigging of aircraft, and a heavy flying programme. There was a lot of sport as well—Malan played rugger, while Tuck took up swimming and fencing.

In Tuck's view, Malan was a very experienced fighter pilot who knew his job inside out, a damned good fighter leader in the air, jolly good with discipline, had a strong but very pleasant personality—a pilot who flew well and could shoot straight—he was quiet and thoughtful, but would have as much to say as anyone else when it really mattered.

At Grantham, Malan advanced to fly the single-seat Gloster Gauntlet biplane fighter powered by the Bristol Mercury engine. It was the fastest aircraft in the Royal Air Force from 1935 to 1937 and the fighter mainstay of the time. Most RAF pilots, including Malan, liked flying the Gauntlet with its stability and fine aerobatic capabilities. But he recalled a few incidents in 1937 when, as a Flight Lieutenant, the aeroplane had made him sit up straight. During a visit to Ulster on Empire Day, he was leading A Flight across the Irish Channel and his friend, Paddy Treacy, was leading B Flight. They were to give a display of aerobatics, a few rolls and loops. Adolph and Paddy decided when they took off that they could improve on the presentation and Paddy got behind Adolph in a mock dog fight. Malan did a few flick half-rolls which pleased the crowd, but enraged the commanding officer. When the pair landed, the C.O. put them under close arrest—which meant having a guard watching them constantly. The next morning the Belfast *Daily Telegraph* gave Paddy and Adolph high praise for the dogfight and the extra flourishes. This impressed the C.O. sufficiently to make him change his mind and let the two pilots off with no further punishment.

While practising for that display, Adolph had the worst twenty minutes of flying he had experienced up till then. "For twenty minutes I was staring at death. It happened while we were flying north of the aerodrome and well out to sea. [John] Gillan, who was then a Met. Officer and later became a fine fighter pilot, was flying with me at the time, when we lost our way as fog closed down. I knew the sea was right underneath. My petrol was getting lower every minute. I could see nothing ahead. I didn't know how far off the coast still was. For a while I sat up top of Gillan. Then I lost him. I was flying at 0 feet by this time, not more than twenty feet above the waves, and throttled right back. My bowels turned to water. I was sweating like a pig. In fact I had a rash under my arms from that scare for a long time after. I could literally feel the sea coming up to take me. My petrol gauge registered nothing. I'd just about given up hope and was clearing myself ready to jump as I hit the water when a bit of coastline showed through a small gap ahead. I managed to clear the rocks and force-land on some nice green grass that turned out to be Lord Antrim's private golf course."

On completion of the advanced training at Grantham, Adolph was posted to No 74 Squadron which was then stationed at Hornchurch, Essex. It was there that a former Royal Navy officer heard that Malan had acquired the nickname "Admiral" while at Grantham. When the ex-Navy man learned that Adolph had actually been Royal Naval Reserve rather than Royal Navy, he began calling Adolph "Sailor" and the moniker stuck.

In those early, relatively quiet days at Hornchurch, Sailor put in what flight time he could in the Gauntlet. "To pass the time, someone bet me I couldn't take the Gauntlet up and do a roll off the top at hangar height. It was a law that you don't stunt over the airfield. But the O.C. was away at the time and I knew this Gauntlet and what it could do. It was a perfect machine in which to do a flick half-turn, and you could fly it on its side with perfect safety, although the movement looked as if you were bound to go into a dangerous spin. I took the Gauntlet up and had a lovely time turning it inside out. Unfortunately, the C.O. returned unexpectedly and saw me. I then had to report to his office for an offence that could warrant a court-martial. He was storming with rage. He finished up: 'I won't have it, Malan. Get out of my office.' And then, as I was thankfully preparing to go, he said, in a different voice: 'But, you know, I like people to do it.'

KIWI

Many years after the Second World War, Sailor's wartime friend and fellow Battle of Britain Spitfire pilot, Al Deere recalled: "It was a glorious summer's day, and the little New Zealand town of Westport, at the foot of the Southern Alps, was bathed in the nice warm sunshine. Three little barefooted boys were crouched around a circular patch of clay engrossed in a game of marbles. As they played, a new and puzzling sound gradually intruded upon their little world, faintly at first but growing louder and more insistent, until it filled the air with a strange persistent throb. Almost simultaneously, three little heads jerked upwards and three pairs of eyes gazed skywards seeking an answer to this unwanted intrusion. One glance was sufficient; a tiny bi-plane droned overhead, its whirling propeller glinting in the bright sun.

"To three small boys, whose only contact with this mechanical bird had been through the medium of picture books and models, this was an event of the first importance. That aeroplanes could fly was never in doubt; the fact that one was now overhead seemed unbelievable. Where did it come from? Who was the pilot? Where was it going to land? The latter question was soon answered by a change in course as the aeroplane, having first circled the town, headed off in the direction of the coast with the obvious intention of landing on the long, firm stretch of sand which fringed the water's edge. Discussion and agreement were unnecessary; with one accord the three set off on a four-mile run to the beach. As the youngest of those three boys—the others were my elder brothers—I was hard pressed to keep up. With each sobbing breath I willed myself to keep going knowing that should I falter no compassion would be shown, and I would be left behind.

"At last we were there. Before us stood the small silver biplane surrounded by a knot of curious sightseers many of whom were, no doubt, seeing an aeroplane for the very first time at close range. Feverishly my eyes sought for the figure of someone who measured up to my childish ideal of what a pilot should look like; alas, no tall, helmeted and gloved individual was to be seen. The pilot had been driven off in a waiting motor-car.

"For long hours we stood and gazed in silent wonder at the aeroplane until eventually our persistence was rewarded by an invitation to look into the cockpit. There within easy reach was the 'joy stick' as it was then called, the very sound of the word conjuring up dreams of looping and rolling in the blue heavens. And there, too, above a fascinating row of tiny dials, was the speedometer, the only instrument I could recognize.

"As I gazed at these innermost secrets of the pilot's cockpit, there gradually grew within me a resolve that one day I would fly a machine like this and, perhaps, land on this very beach to the envy and delight of my boyhood friends. That night in bed I could think of nothing else, and for many weeks afterwards my desire to fly was fed with boyish imagination until the seed, which had been sewn from the moment I first sighted the aeroplane, firmly took root."

During his illustrious World War Two combat career, Al Deere was credited with the destruction of seventeen enemy aircraft. In his foreword to Deere's 1959 autobiography *Nine Lives*, Air Chief Marshal Lord Dowding wrote: "Alan Deere must have had an exceptionally efficient Guardian Angel who, even so, must have been hard put to it to extricate his charge from the apparently hopeless predicaments in which he was constantly finding himself.

"It is perhaps as a treatise on Courage that this book is principally noteworthy. In two wars I have had the grim opportunities of seeing human endeavour stretched to its

limits—and sometimes beyond. I was commanding the
Fighter Wing in France before and during the Battle of the
Somme in 1916; and there a pilot's or air-gunner's average
expectation of life was one month, and at that time there were
no rest periods for tired and depleted squadrons.

"During the Battle of Britain I was farther away from the
fighting squadrons, and too desperately busy to do much visiting; but I shall never forget the pall of gloom under which
each day's casualties were scanned.

"Even after all these years I can scarcely bear to be brought
back to the atmosphere of those days because of the almost
intolerable memory of stress and sadness which it engenders.

"People are apt to talk of a very brave man as if his courage
were some sort of Divine Dispensation which prevented his
ever feeling afraid; but I have yet to meet the man who never
in his heart knew the fear of death or, perhaps worse, of muti-
lation.

"The brave man never lets his fear be seen, never permits
his mind to dwell aimlessly on present or future dangers and
never allows his actions to be influenced by his fears.

"Of course the bravest nature can in the course of time be
undermined by battling with inferior material against superi-
or numbers and by lack of opportunities for sleep and rest,
and we see this process at times wearing down even Alan
Deere's endurance; he never cracked—perhaps his was one
of those rugged characters which never would crack this side
of death; and relief came just in time.

"Alan Deere will always stand to me as an example of the
best type of Fighter Pilot whose endurance and determination brought this country of ours through the greatest immediate danger which has threatened it since Napoleon's armies
stood along the Channel shore. May Britain and the
Commonwealth never lack such sons."

In his instruction on service aircraft at No. 6 Flying Training

School, Netheravon, Al Deere first flew the Hawker Hart, which he described as an obsolete but wonderful old bi-plane. "I made good progress but one incident nearly put paid to my career in the RAF I was not feeling too well after a rugger celebration the night before, when my instructor, rather a quick-tempered individual, set me the exercise of 'Spins under the hood recovering on instruments on a set heading.' To spin the aircraft first one way and then the other, under a hood which blotted out all but my instrument panel, and to recover from the spin with the aircraft pointing in a pre-determined direction was difficult at any time but impossible for me that day. The instructor's exasperated voice came over the inter-communication: 'If you think you will ever be a pilot let alone a fighter pilot, you are very much mistaken. I've had enough of your futile attempts on this trip, and there is no point in carrying on with the exercise.'

"Till this day I don't know what made me see red, perhaps my own futility combined with the hangover, but see red I did and promptly shouted back, 'I'm damn well fed up too, why don't you get in this seat and have a go yourself?'

"There was no reply, and I don't think I expected one. About five minutes later we landed back at base and taxied to dispersal where the instructor said, 'You can come out of there now, Deere. Report to me in the flight commander's office in five minutes.'

" 'This,' I thought, 'is where Acting Pilot Officer Alan Deere says good-bye to a career as a pilot in the Royal Air Force.' My conduct was inexcusable and I knew it. I really felt miserable and roundly cursed myself for letting my outspokenness, a trait no doubt inherited from my Irish ancestors, get out of hand.

" 'Deere, you've been a stupid young fool and I don't quite know what to do about it,' said my flight commander before whom I stood rigidly at attention.

" 'I am sorry, sir. I apologize, and assure you it won't happen again.'

" 'All right. You will have another chance. It is only because the Royal Air Force has already spent so much money on your training that I am persuaded to be so lenient. Remember though, there will be no second chance and on the next occasion, should there be one, you will be up before the Chief Flying Instructor who will be much more severe. You can go, and don't let it happen again.'

"A very chastened young New Zealander left that office full of good resolutions which, I am pleased to record, were not broken."

It was on his posting to 54 Squadron, then stationed at RAF Hornchurch in Essex, that Deere first met Sailor Malan. "Pilot Officer Arthur Charrett, a Canadian, was posted to 54 Squadron with me, and we travelled to Hornchurch together. Art it was who christened me 'Al,' a nickname or sort of half-name, which has stuck throughout my service career. It was thus he referred to me in our early days at Hornchurch, and my fellow officers there were not aware that it wasn't my full Christian name, and followed suit.

"My first sight of Hornchurch, seen through the carriage windows as the train approached Elm Park, the nearest station to the airfield, was of three large hangars rising out of a sea of houses in the heavily built-up area which surrounded the small grass airfield of First World War vintage, when it was known as Sutton's Farm.

"It was a great disappointment to find on our arrival at Station Headquarters that 54 Squadron was on block leave and that the pilots were not due to return for another two weeks. To a suggestion that we take a few more days leave, Art and I were not responsive, for reasons of finance. It was decided therefore that we would be temporarily attached to

No. 74 Squadron which, with No. 65 Squadron, made an operational strength of three squadrons on the station. I was sent to 'A' Flight commanded by 'Sailor' Malan, later to prove an outstanding pilot in the war and at that time leader of the flight which was to win the Sassoon Cup for flight attacks. 'Sailor,' who had been in the Merchant Navy, was older than most of his colleagues and a married man. He was most considerate towards me and although he couldn't give me much flying, because of the demands of his own pilots, he did allow me to get airborne in a Gloster Gauntlet fighter with which his squadron was equipped. We later became very firm friends and to this day exchange letters."

In March 1943, Deere was posted to Biggin Hill as Wing Leader under Sailor who was then station commander at the base. Again, Sailor showed his regard for Al, expressing his complete confidence in him and allowing him to introduce some new tactics to employ while leading the Wing. Deere's ideas included having all the squadrons and sections of the Wing operate independently. He planned to lead the Wing with complete control over the formation, the routes and timings in operations. He let the squadron and section leaders use their own discretion in the event of enemy attacks, with the proviso that they had to inform him before going into action. He insisted that all the squadrons take equal responsibility when his Wing was acting as escort on a raid, and be prepared to take over the lead should the other squadrons be engaged in combat. Finally, he determined that the fighters of the Wing were not to be restricted by their role as escorts to bombers. It was a lesson learned during the Battle of Britain when German fighter escorts were disastrously required to stay with the bombers they were shepherding. Deere's Spitfires, while having been ordered to always be within sight of the bombers they were escorting, would not be required to stick with those much slower aircraft in combat.

Al always worked well with Sailor in their days together at Biggin Hill. It was a partnership enriched by the enormous respect and admiration they had for each other.

SPITFIRE

Rumble thy bellyful!' Spit, fire! spout, rain!'
—Shakespeare, King Lear, Act three, scene two.

Sailor married Lynda Fraser in 1938. That September an
international crisis developed when German Chancellor
Adolf Hitler threatened war with Czechoslovakia unless it
immediately ceded the Sudetenland, an area settled mainly
by ethnic Germans, to Germany. As the Czechs had formed
military alliances with France and the Soviet Union, a new
world war seemed to be a strong possibility, but one that the
British Prime Minister, Neville Chamberlain, thought he
could head off by negotiating with Hitler. The policy of
appeasement was established. In that dramatic year it was
becoming clear to many in Britain, and in the Royal Air
Force in particular, that German preparations for war were
advancing on a large and sophisticated scale. Chamberlain
flew to Munich to parlay with the German chancellor and
Italian premier Benito Mussolini played mediator in the pro-
ceedings. An agreement was reached (without Czech partic-
ipation) in which Hitler received the Sudetenland in return
for a non-aggression note which Chamberlain waved at the
press on his return to London, claiming to have achieved
"peace in our time."

Another momentous event for Sailor happened that year
when 74 Squadron was re-equipped with Spitfires, the beautiful new fighter from Vickers-Supermarine. Sailor and
Paddy Treacy took delivery of two new Mark 1s at the
Eastleigh factory. "It was like changing over from Noah's Ark
to the *Queen Mary*. The Spitfire had style and was obviously
a killer. We knew that from the moment when we first fired
our eight guns on a ground target. Moreover, she was a per-

fect lady. She had no vices. She was beautifully positive. You could dive till your eyes were popping out of your head, but the wings would still be there—till your inside melted, and she would still answer to a touch."

They could all see it coming. The men of the British Air Ministry, the leadership of the Royal Air Force, those at the top of government, the captains of Britain's aviation industry, the pilots of Fighter Command, and the majority of the British public. In the second half of the 1930s the spectre of a new and more terrifying war with Germany was overtaking them and they were unready; people rarely are prepared for war unless they intend to make it. There were plenty of indications that the Germans were getting ready for one. There was evidence of a substantial military build- up, a significant increase in martial rhetoric from the Nazi leadership, credible reports from Allied spies, travellers, and visitors to Germany, including Sailor, and importantly, the first practical testing of new German bomber and fighter aircraft in the Spanish Civil War, between July 1936 and April 1939.

One who certainly appreciated the German threat was Supermarine chief designer Reginald J. Mitchell. When Mitchell set out to create the Spitfire, he believed that only a truly superior fighter capability could save Britain if she was attacked from the air. By the 1930s it was clear that aviation would have a fundamental role in the next war. In the Spitfire, he gave the British nation an edge, though he didn't live to see the plane in the magnificent part it played— together with the Hawker Hurricane—during the Battle of Britain in the summer and fall of 1940.

The Air Ministry had put out a call in 1930 to the British aviation industry for a new single seat monoplane day and night fighter capable of at least 195 mph, with exceptional manoeuvrability, considerable range, high initial rate of climb, a low landing speed, and good visibility for the pilot. The armament was to be four .303 Vickers machine-guns and the aircraft was to be fitted with a radio/telephone. The aeroplane makers Westland, Blackburn, Bristol, Gloster, and Supermarine all prepared designs for the specification. Their efforts were unsuccessful and the Supermarine aeroplane, the Type 224, was a great disappointment for Mitchell. In the end, the Air Ministry had no choice but to adopt the Gloster Gladiator biplane for its next fighter. Mitchell then began work on revising the design of the Type 224, incorporating many important refinements including a retractable under-carriage and a much thinner wing. In time it began to resemble the first Spitfire. It was in the summer of 1933 that his cancer was diagnosed.

Early in 1936 the prototype fighter, serial number K5054, was approaching completion and as the time for the maiden flight grew near, so did the time to name the plane. Shrike and Shrew were among the suggested names. Sir Robert McLean, however, was adamant that it should be called Spitfire, a name that had already been used for the ill-fated Type 224 and was, therefore, not favoured by many in the Supermarine organisation. For some it was a bad omen, one associated with failure.

Mitchell himself thought it a "silly" name. At least three ships of the Royal Navy had born the name HMS *Spitfire*, one of them, a destroyer, had taken part in the Battle of Jutland in the First World War. Given the timing, though, the most likely origin of the name is the 1934 Katharine Hepburn movie, *Spitfire*. Fortunately, McLean prevailed, to the enthusiastic approval of millions of Spitfire lovers the world over.

Jeffrey Quill, chief Supermarine test pilot: "Popular folk-lore has it that the first flight of the Spitfire was on 5 March

1936, but I flew Mutt [Summers, test pilot for the Spitfire programme at Supermarine] to Eastleigh for the particular purpose of making that first flight on 6 March." At 4:35 pm Summers took the little fighter up and landed it eight minutes later with an admonition to those gathered round it, 'I don't want anything touched.' He flew it again the next day for twenty-three minutes. The concensus at Supermarine was that the aeroplane was good, but needed work. With a top speed of only 330 mph, it was no faster than its nearest rival, the five-month-old Hawker Hurricane fighter prototype, which was also Merlin-powered. In February 1937, R. J. Mitchell's doctors told that him he had only four or five months to live. He died on June 11th.

One who deserves credit for helping spearhead the development of the Spitfire, the Hawker Hurricane, and the radio direction finding radar system, all of which led to RAF victory in the Battle of Britain, is Air Chief Marshal Sir Hugh Dowding. Dowding had been a flight commander with the Royal Flying Corps in the First World War and was later appointed to the Air Council for Supply and Research, where he was able to exert maximum support for the weaponry that won the day in 1940.

The Spitfire was the only Allied fighter to remain in both full production and front-line operational service throughout the Second World War. Delivery of the first Mk Is, to No 19 Squadron at Duxford, began on August 6th 1938. That initial Air Ministry order for 310 Spitfires was followed by orders for three more batches totalling an additional 950 aircraft. By the outbreak of the war on September 3rd 1939, nine RAF squadrons had been equipped with Spitfires. And by the start of the Battle of Britain in July 1940, Air Chief Marshal Dowding had equipped nineteen squadrons of Fighter Command with Spitfires.

The Mark I Spitfire, equipping Sailor Malan's outfit was truly impressive, a great advance over anything the RAF had previously operated. It could climb at a rate of more than 2,000 feet a minute, had a top speed of 362 miles per hour at an altitude of 18,500 feet and a service ceiling of 31,900 feet. It was armed with eight .303 Browning machine-guns with a firepower of 9,600 rounds a minute. Sailor: "You fix the range on the ground. 250 yards is the deadliest. The idea behind this armament is that each gun has its own little place in the heaven. By a criss-cross of fire, ranged at a selected distance, you achieve the maximum lethal pattern."

Fortunately for Sailor and the other Spitfire pilots in the Battle of Britain, the respite provided by the Phoney War period from September 1939 to May 1940 enabled Vickers-Supermarine to add many refinements to Mitchell's lovely killer. They included armour plating protection under and behind the pilot's seat, a three-blade constant-speed propeller, the adoption of 100 octane petrol for the Merlin engine, added protection around the fuel tank, and a sturdier glass windscreen, all of which made the Spitfire much better prepared for the imminent air battle.

As the war situation in France deteriorated, the RAF Hurricanes that had been sent there to contend with the advancing enemy were finally recalled to England. Again to the credit of Air Chief Marshal Dowding, no Spitfires had been utilised in the Battle of France. Dowding was determined that all the available Spitfires would be retained in England for the protection of Britain when the great air campaign he was expecting came that summer. He had been busy during the Phoney War period, establishing his air defence system of radar installations, airfields, aircraft, pilots, the Observer Corps, barrage balloons and anti-aircraft batteries. In his powerful memo of April 18th 1940 to the Under Secretary for Air, he wrote: "I believe that if an adequate fighter force is kept in this country, if the Fleet remains in being, and if the Home Forces are suitably organised to resist invasion, we should be able to carry on the war single- handed for some time, if not indefinitely. But, if the Home Defence Force is drained away in desperate attempts to remedy the situation in France, defeat in France will lead to the final, complete and irremediable defeat of this Country."

The wartime test pilots Jeffrey Quill and Alex Henshaw probably knew more about flying the Spitfire than anyone. Henshaw, the chief test pilot at the new Castle Bromwich, Birmingham, Spitfire factory between 1940 and 1946, flew all marks of the plane, a total of 2,360 Spitfires and Seafires, more than ten per cent of the entire production.

After a thorough pre-flight check, Henshaw would take off and, once at circuit height, he would trim the aircraft and try to get her to fly straight and level with hands off the stick. Once the trim was satisfactory he would take the Spitfire up in a full-throttle climb at 2,850 rpm to the rated altitude of one or both supercharger blowers. Then he would make a careful check of the power output from the engine, calibrated for height and temperature. If all appeared satisfactory he would then put her into a dive at full power and 3,000 rpm, and trim her to fly hands and feet off at 460 mph indicated air speed. He never cleared a Spitfire unless he had carried out a few aerobatic tests to determine how good or bad she was. The production test was usually quite a brisk affair: the initial circuit lasted less than ten minutes and the main flight took between twenty and thirty minutes. Then the aircraft received a final once-over by the ground mechanics, any faults were rectified and the Spitfire was ready for collection.

Henshaw loved the Spitfire in all her many versions, But said that the later marks, although they were faster than the earlier ones, were also much heavier and so did not handle as well. One did not have such positive control over them.

One test of manoeuvrability was to throw her into a flick-roll and see how many times she rolled. "With the Mark II or the Mark V one got two-and-a-half flick-rolls, but the Mark IX was heavier and you got only one-and-a-half. With the later and still heavier versions, one got even less. The essence of aircraft design is compromise, and an improvement at one end of the performance envelope is rarely achieved without a deterioration somewhere else."

And what of the opposition? The main adversary that the Spitfire faced in its World War Two combat career was the Messerschmitt Me and Bf 109s. The 109 was designed by Willy Messerschmitt and Robert Lusser and were the most produced fighter aircraft in history with a total of 33,984 built by April 1945. They were flown by Germany's three highest scoring fighter aces of WW2, claiming a total of 928 victories among them. It was operated on the western front, the eastern front, in the North African campaign, and by other air forces during and/or following WW2, including Bulgaria, Croatia, the Republic of China, Czechoslovakia, Finland, Hungary, Israel, Italy, Romania, the Slovak Republic, Spain, Switzerland, and Yugoslavia.

The 109 resulted from a 1933 *Reichsluftfahrtministerium* requirement for a new single seat fighter plane. It was to have a top speed of 250 mph at 19,690 feet—to be reached in no more than seventeen minutes, a total flight duration of ninety minutes, and an operational ceiling of 32,500 feet. It would be powered initially by the Junkers Jumo 210 aero engine, and later by the Daimler Benz DB 600 series engines. The plane featured easy access to the engine, the fuselage weapons and other systems, as well as automatically-opening wing leading-edge slats to increase the overall lift of the wing and improve low-speed performance.

The new German fighter was introduced to the world at the

1936 Berlin Olympics when the prototype of the 109 was flown. The new 109E first entered service with the "Condor Legion" in the Spanish Civil War and was the mainstay of the Luftwaffe fighter force through the middle of 1941 when it was replaced by the 109F. The Bf 109 also served as an escort fighter during the Battle of Britain. In the course of the war, its pilots achieved more kills than those of any other fighter type. 105 Bf 109 pilots were credited with more than one hundred enemy aircraft downed; thirteen of them achieved more than 200 kills and two of them scored more than 300. Those 105 pilots were credited with a total of nearly 15,000 aerial victories.

How did the Bf 109 compare to the Spitfire? In its favour the German fighter was cheaper and easier to build, service and maintain, but it was not quite as finely crafted as the British plane. The Spitfire, with its elegant compound curves, was also designed for purpose and likely with the concept that 'if it looks right, it will fly right' in mind. Certainly, few aircraft in aviation history have looked as right as the lovely Spitfire.

Both the Bf 109 and the Spitfire were extremely effective in their roles, though both had definite limitations. In the heat of aerial combat it could be more than a little disconcerting when a diving Spitfire pilot, manoeuvring his aircraft for a shot at his opponent, experienced sudden engine failure. In negative-g situations the Merlin engine's SU carburettor suffered fuel loss and the engine cut out. It restarted within a few seconds, but in the critical engagements of the Battle of Britain it was dangerous and frustrating when, in aligning for a kill, the engine spluttered and vital seconds were lost as the pilot was forced to either do a half-roll or throw the plane on its back to restore the fuel flow. With its fuel-injected Daimler Benz engine, the 109 had no such trouble.

The Spitfire carburettor problem was ultimately solved by Beatrice 'Tilly' Shilling, a scientist at the Royal Aircraft Establishment, Farnborough. She found that drilling a small hole through a metal diaphragm over the float chambers of the carburettor overcame the performance flaw. Her solution was known around the RAF as 'Miss Shilling's Orifice', and was employed until Rolls-Royce developed an anti-g version of the carburettor.

Former Bf 109 pilots I have talked with, while liberally praising the capabilities of their wartime machine, expressed a common regret about the design of the tiny cockpit and canopy. All had lost fellow 109 pilots to the difficulty in getting out of the fighter in an emergency. Most agreed too that the Spitfire, with its highly efficient elliptical wing, could easily outturn the 109 in the extremes of a dogfight. In his book *Spitfire The Biography* author Jonathan Glancey explained: "Because the angle the Spitfire wing presents to the airflow is greater nearer the fuselage, where the wing is much thicker, than it is towards the thin wingtip, the pilot would feel an impending stall as a slight wobble well before the wings themselves stalled. This was particularly important in combat as, in a tight turn and on full throttle, the aircraft needed to be kept just on the edge of stalling to achieve the minimum turning circle. This made the Spitfire an extremely safe and forgiving aircraft to fly, allowing the pilots to make extremely tight turns and so outmanoeuvre their opponents."

The similarity of their performance meant that the outcome of a dogfight depended heavily on whether one or the other pilot was a really good shot. Marksmanship often counted for more than flying skill. The best and highest scoring fighter pilots of WW2 were those who combined a natural shooting skill with the ability and willingness to get in so close to the opponent that a kill was virtually assured. The pilots like Sailor Malan and those who followed his example, could trace their success in combat both to being excellent shots and their discipline in resisting the temptation to follow an enemy aircraft after they had damaged it. Those who yielded to that temptation were often "bounced" by an enemy fighter they never saw and were killed for their carelessness.

The highest scoring German pilots flew many more operations than their RAF counterparts and so had many more opportunities to increase their scores. The fighter pilots of the Luftwaffe were required to fly combat until they were seriously wounded, killed, or the war ended, unlike RAF fighter pilots who were occasionally stood down for a rest, training or other assignments.

A severe limitation faced by the pilots of both Spitfires and Bf 109s was the relatively short range of both aircraft. With all the years of their development through the late 1930s, the Second World War, and after, neither plane was developed into a truly long-range fighter. Only the unarmed photo-reconnaissance versions of the Spitfire and 109 were capable of flying long-range missions. The Spitfire was designed to be a defensive weapon, defending Britain over Britain from enemy raiders. The 109 was deployed in the Battle of Britain mainly from forward fields in France in sorties to southeastern England where they were limited to about ten minutes combat time before having to return to base to be refuelled. Thus, while they were superb fighters in many respects, both the Spitfire and Bf 109's offensive mission capabilities were measured in minutes rather than hours.

In late September 1940, as the end of the Battle neared, it was clear to Hitler that his Luftwaffe was not going to achieve control of the air over the British Isles and he was forced to sideline Sea Lion, his plan for invading England. The Spitfires and Hurricanes of Fighter Command had done their work with efficiency and, vitally, Britain was preserved to become a massive operational base for the heavy strategic bombers of the RAF and the U.S. Eighth Air Force in their round-the-clock campaign against targets in Nazi Germany and German-held Europe.

As K5054, the prototype Spitfire, neared completion in February 1936, a quick tally of the costs incurred to date showed: Supermarine—£14,637, or roughly £600,000 in today's money; Rolls-Royce—£7,500; and government funding—£12,478, a steal by any measure. The cost to the Air Ministry for each production Spitfire of the first batch of 300+ aeroplanes was £9,500.

The last production Spitfire rolled from the factory in February 1948. By then, 20,351 Spitfires had been built. Spitfires were still operational in the air force until the 1950s. It was the only British fighter in continuous production before, during and after the Second World War.

The iconic Spitfire of WW2 lives on today. Around seventy airworthy examples remain in the care of their appreciative, enthusiastic owners. The machines frequently appear in air displays around the world, bringing thrills to thousands, and the unforgettable sight and sound of the best of the best of pilot's aeroplanes.

HORNCHURCH

Sailor Malan was in good company at RAF Hornchurch, home to his No 74 Squadron 'Tigers.' The squadron shared the field with Nos 54 and 65 Squadrons, whose numbers included some pilots who would be among the most celebrated high achievers of the Second World War—Al Deere, Robert Stanford Tuck, Colin Gray, and in No 74 Squadron, H.M. Stephen, and John Colin Mungo-Park. Mungo-Park used to bring Sailor and some of the other pilots of 74 home with him when they went on leave. He and Stephen formed a highly effective air combat team in the Battle of Britain, and by the end of the Battle, Mungo-Park had been credited with twelve enemy aircraft destroyed. Sadly, his luck ran out on June 27th, 1941, when he was leading eleven Spitfires from the squadron's base at Biggin Hill, escorting a formation of bombers on a raid to a target in northern France. Bounced by German fighters, Mungo-Park's aircraft was set on fire. A teenage boy near the Belgian coast saw the Spitfire rapidly descending and trailing dense black smoke before it crashed near the town of De Panne. The boy and his companions rode their bicycles to the crash site which they saw was being guarded by German troops. Mungo-Park's body lay beside the crushed fuselage. He was twenty-three when he died.

Sailor: "Our first real scare came in September 1938 after the Munich climb down. We flew to Hornchurch in bad fog, and the Station Commander ordered everybody—pilots and all—to get hold of paint-brushes and camouflage the planes. Patrols in formation were started. My squadron was 'at readiness'. From that time till war came we were more or less continuously on a war footing."

September 3rd, 1939. War declared. Sailor didn't write home much. It was a rare occasion when he sat down in the officer's Mess to write a note to his parents. The evening of September 4th: "I started to write this letter to you over a week ago but the same day we were ordered to readiness and war stations and I hadn't another chance. I suppose I am in the prime of life and yet I have a lot to be thankful for. I have had quite a good fling for one. But the biggest factor is that I have had eighteen months of complete happiness and blissful contentment with one of the sweetest women in the world, and thank God for that. It probably seems a strange thing to say but I am more ready to enter the conflict having had those eighteen glorious months." There was a four-day pause before he resumed writing: "The Spitfire is a formidable machine and they will get a most unpleasant shock if they come over here. We are quite ready for them."

Unidentified aircraft were reported to be approaching from the east over the West Mersea at a little after six a.m. on September 6th, 1939. The RAF ground controllers quickly ordered six Hurricane fighters of No 56 Squadron scrambled from their base at North Weald in Essex. Their commander, Group Captain D.F. Lucking, also despatched the remaining aircraft of his squadron, and unknown to Lucking and his pilots, two further Hurricane pilots took off as reserves. More Hurricanes, these from No 151 Squadron, also from North Weald, as well as several Spitfires from Nos 54, 65 and 74 Squadrons at Hornchurch, were also scrambled to meet the apparent enemy threat.

The war had been going for only three days and none of the RAF pilots flying this day had yet seen a German aircraft. No proper identification system for pilots to distinguish between friendly and enemy aircraft had as yet been devised and communications between ground command centres and aircraft in the air were poor. Conditions were ripe for a cock-up and, for 74 Squadron, it would be an inauspicious start to their World War Two combat history. For Sailor, in particular, it would be a stressful beginning.

He was in command of the squadron's A Flight and, when his pilots sighted what they believed to be the enemy planes, after a series of likely misunderstandings, Sailor ordered them to attack the Germans, sending Flying Officer Vincent 'Paddy' Byrne and Pilot Officer John Freeborn to put their Spitfires on target and open fire. The primitive radar plots of the day had given a confused message. The 'enemy aircraft' were incorrectly identified and were, in fact, Hurricanes of No 56 Squadron returning from an operation. One of them, an aircraft piloted by Flying Officer Frank Rose, was shot down but Rose survived. A second Hurricane, that of Pilot Officer Montague Hulton-Harrop, was struck by the bullets of John Freeborn. Hulton-Harrop received a wound in the back of the head and died as his fighter crashed at Manor Farm near Hintlesham, Suffolk, about five miles west of Ipswich. His was the first aircraft to be shot down by a Spitfire and he was the first British pilot fatality of the war.

The air raid warning had been a false alarm, the RAF Hurricanes and Spitfires had been scrambled in error and the unfortunate "friendly fire" incident a tragic mistake. It was thereafter referred to as the Battle of Barking Creek.

On returning from the flight, pilots Byrne and Freeborn and Group Captain Lucking were all placed under close arrest. In the subsequent court-martial that was held at Fighter Command Headquarters, Bentley Priory, Freeborn believed that his C.O., Sailor Malan, was trying to duck responsibility for the incident. Sailor testified against his pilots in the hearing, indicating that Freeborn had been impetuous and irresponsible and may have misinterpreted or misheard the final order which he, Malan, had given, insisting he had issued a recall order prior to the accidental downing of the planes. Freeborn's counsel called Malan a barefaced liar. The court found both Freeborn and Byrne innocent and ruled the case an unfortunate accident of war. The authorities took pains to hush up the entire event at the time, but word spread quickly through the air force and, in a positive twist, the inadequacies of the RAF radar and aircraft identification procedures were exposed. The system was reviewed and then greatly improved.

John Freeborn, who died August 28th, 2010, flew more hours during the Battle of Britain than any other RAF pilot. He was involved in the air fighting over Dunkirk in May 1940 and was forced down on the beach near Calais when his Spitfifre was badly damaged. On August 11th he flew four sorties and was credited with shooting down three enemy fighters and probably downing a fourth. By the end of November he had been on the squadron longer than any other pilot. Though he had been exonerated in the death of Hulton-Harrop in 1939, the incident stayed with him for the rest of his life. Shortly before his own death he commented: "I think about him nearly every day. I always have done. I've had a good life—and he should have had a good life too."

Group Captain Lucking lost his command position with 56 Squadron. Frank Rose was killed in action over Vitry en Artoise, France, on May 18th, 1940. Montague Hulton-Harrop was buried at St Andrew's Church, North Weald. Sailor Malan went on to become one of the greatest fighter pilots and air leaders of the war.

In the 1950s, Air Chief Marshal Lord Dowding wrote in his forward for Alan Deere's book *Nine Lives*: "I refer to the Battle of Barking Creek . . . The large radar stations of the R.D.F. Chain, as it was then called, were capable of giving plots of aircraft both to the east and to the west, but would give precisely the same indication for each. As they were intended to plot tracks to the eastward only, an electrical 'screen' was installed to smother all echoes from the westward. Aircraft flying inland were plotted either by the

Observer Corps or the Sector Operations Rooms.

"What happened on this occasion was that a refugee air-craft from Holland flew in without due notice and a section was sent off to intercept. The electrical screen at Canewdon R.D.F. Station had somehow failed and this section appeared on the screen as coming from the east.

"More aircraft were sent up to meet this non-existent attack, and more again to intercept them. Finally the table was covered with plots of incoming raids and yet no bomb had been dropped nor had any raid been picked up by the Observer Corps on reaching the coastline.

"His Majesty the King had chosen this inopportune time to honour my Headquarters with a visit, and I fear that he must have found me a most distrait host, for I was itching to find out what it was that had gone wrong."

Equipped with new Spitfires, Sailor and the pilots of No 74 engaged aircraft of the German Air Force over Dunkirk on May 21st 1940. "I saw black puffs about 15,000 feet over Calais. The ack-ack guns kept firing and that meant there were Jerries about. I yelled 'Tally-ho, over Calais. Let's cut some cake.' " He scored his first victories there, destroying a Ju 88 fighter-bomber, a Heinkel He 111 bomber, and dam-aging another Ju 88. "I'd tasted blood at last. The release from tension was terrific, the thrill enormous. I had been wondering for so long—too long—how I'd react in my first show. Now I knew. Everything I had learnt had come right. There was hardly time to feel even scared." The next day he shared in the destruction of a Ju 88 and on May 24th he downed a He 111 and shared in the destruction of a Do 17. His final combat over Dunkirk came on the 27th when he shot down a Bf 109 fighter, shared in the downing of a Do 17 and damaged two more. For these actions Sailor was award-ed the Distinguished Flying Cross on June 11th, and on the

18th he shot down two He 111s during a night operation. Sailor: "The first letter of congratulation that I received came from an insurance company, a firm whose correspondence used to frighten me because the only time they ever wrote to me was when I was behind with my premiums. This time they never mentioned a word about any money owing."

With the opening round of the Battle of Britain in July, Sailor shared in the destruction of an He 111 on the 12th, was credited with the probable destruction of a Bf 109 on the 19th, and damaged another Bf 109 on the 25th.

Sunday, July 28th. Sailor was leading twelve Spitfires of 74 Squadron out of Manston in Kent when they encountered four *staffeln* of Messerschmitt 109s over the English Channel. The German fighters were from JG 51, commanded by their great ace, Werner Mölders, on his first day as their leader. Closing on the enemy aircraft, Malan selected the lead element of the formation, manoeuvred into position, fired and watched as his victim went down. Mölders then turned, got position on one of the Spitfires and quickly shot it down. It was the German commander's 129th combat mission of the war and his twenty-sixth kill. He then turned on Malan and in a few seconds was aligned for a shot, but Sailor reacted quickly, racking the Spitfire over as tightly as he could until he was able to bring the German into his own sights. He then raked the Messerschmitt with bullets, wounding the pilot. Mölders was able to nurse the badly damaged fighter back to his field at Wissant. The wounds to his leg were such that he was hospitalized and out of action for more than a month.

Flight Lieutenant Piers Kelly was posted to No 74 Squadron just as the Battle got under way. He was immediately impressed by Sailor, who always took a great interest in his new pilots, giving the inexperienced men all the advice he could in order to ease their transition to becoming fighter pilots. Kelly was extemely grateful for this consideration, knowing he needed all the help he could get. He found Sailor a firm disciplinarian who kept all of the squadron's pilots on their toes and never let up on their training. He recalled that, to get all of the aircraft up above cloud while still in formation, Sailor would have them practise flying up through thick cloud in sections, climbing hard, their only reference point being the tailwheel of the Spitfire immediately ahead in the murk. It worked. Once through the cloud cover, Sailor was still leading and all twelve Spitfires were ready for action.

Malan and his pilots met the first German raid of August 13th—*Adler Tag* or Eagle Day—scrambling from Hornchurch at 5:55 a.m. It was out over the Thames Estuary where they ran into a large force of Dornier Do 17s which were heading for the English coast. The Dorniers were unescorted and Kelly recalled that the Tigers of 74 were so eager for a crack at the Germans that they were "elbowing each other out of the way."

From the start of the Battle, Sailor was developing into a superb tactician as well. His advanced, enlightened, frequently unconventional ideas about air fighting soon drew the interest of his air force superiors and some high-ranking government officials, including Prime Minister Churchill. In July Sailor began to disregard Fighter Command's traditional formations and aerial combat tactics. He abandoned the standard three-aircraft vic formation in favour of the "finger-four" formation pioneered by the fighter pilots of the Luftwaffe before the start of the war. He often sought conversations with the Air Vice-Marshal Keith Park, Air Officer-Commanding, 11 Group, on battle tactics. Sailor's efforts ultimately changed Fighter Command into an up-to-date fighting force, ridding it of the old, set-pattern attacks and "tight display" formations of the 1930s. He believed it

essential that one had to get in quite close to an enemy aircraft before opening fire at it, and had the guns of his Spitfire
re-aligned and harmonized to a convergence distance of 250
yards instead of the recommended 400. Many pilots of his
squadron, and others in Fighter Command, as well as in the
fighter squadrons of the American air force, later followed
his lead.

Always conscious too of Sailor's approach to discipline and
of his perfectionist view of all his men's work, was the fitter
who maintained his personal aircraft: "Having spent
many hours patching up his Spitfire [to be] ready for the next
trip, I could well realize the marvellous escapes he must
have had. Although his Spitfire would come back battered
each time, he would not part with it in exchange for a new
and more modern one. His instructions to his crew were: 'My
machine has got to be serviceable. There can be absolutely
no excuse.' His engine had to go the first time, the radio-telephone just had to function even if his junior pilots' radios
failed at times. And his guns weren't allowed to have stop-
pages."

Sailor was promoted to Acting Squadron Leader and given
command of 74 Squadron on August 8th 1940 and his victories continued to mount as the campaign raged. He ran the
unit with the sort of strict, unwavering discipline that the
pilots had come to expect: "Kick their arses once a day and I
have the toughest bunch in Fighter Command."

From Sailor's combat report of August 8th: "I was Dysoe
Leader when squadron was sent off to intercept bandits
approaching Dover at a reported height of 13,000 feet. I
climbed on an E.N.E. course to 20,000 feet into the sun, and
then turned down-sun towards Dover and surprised eight Me
109s at 20,000 feet flying in pairs, staggered line astern

towards Dover. I ordered the squadron to attack. Some of them adopted the usual German fighter evasive tactics, i.e., quick half-roll and dive. On this occasion, as the air seemed clear of German aircraft above us, I followed one down and overtook him after he had dived 2,000 feet, opening fire during the dive at 200 yards' range with deflection. He levelled out at about 12,000 feet, when I gave him two two- second bursts at 100 yards range. He was in a quick half-roll and dived towards the French coast. I closed again to 100 yards' range and gave him another two or three two-second bursts, when he suddenly burst into flames and was obscured by heavy smoke. This was at 4,000 feet, one mile N.W. of Cap Gris Nez. I did not watch him go in, but flew back as fast as I could. I did not observe any of the engagements of the rest of the squadron. N.B.—Normally I have strongly advised all of the pilots in the squadron not to follow 109s on the half-roll and dive because in most cases we are outnumbered, and generally at least one layer of enemy fighters is some thousands of feet above. It was found that even at high altitudes there was no difficulty in overtaking E/A on diving, apart from the physical strain imposed on the body when pulling out."
—A.G. Malan, Squadron Leader, Commanding, No 74 Squadron

For much of the Battle, Sailor led the Tigers from the forward airfield at Manston in Kent, known as "Hell's Corner", where they would fly each day from Hornchurch.

Being closer to the French coast and the enemy airfields gave 74 Squadron a slightly better position, but they were also that much more vulnerable to strafing and bombing attacks by marauding German fighters and bombers. On one occasion when the pilots of 74 landed at Manston after having been involved in a particularly nasty fight with the enemy over the Channel, they were met by their ever-efficient riggers and fitters who quickly set to work preparing the Spitfires for their next sorties. Conspicuously absent, however, were the station armourers, who were required to replenish the ammunition for the planes. Malan was uncharacteristically furious, an emotion he rarely displayed, but when it happened it was fearsome. He grabbed a belt of .303 ammunition and stormed into a nearby air raid shelter. There he hit the first armourer he found with it and yelled for them all to get out and re-arm the squadron. They were holding up the war effort and he, by God, was not having it.

With August came the next phase of the Battle—the Luftwaffe attacked the key airfields of Fighter Command, and in that month, the arrival on 74 Squadron of two Polish pilots, Flight Lieutenant Stanislaw Brzezina and Flying Officer Henryk Szczesny, Their fellow pilots immediately began calling them "Breezy" and "Sneezy", there being little likelihood of learning the correct pronunciation of the Polish names. In October, after brief stints at Wittering, Coltishall, and Kirton-in-Lindsay, the squadron was relocated to Biggin Hill. There, both of the Polish pilots served the squadron with distinction and Sneezy flew as Sailor's Number Two many times. He and Sailor got along well, both of them being somewhat older than the other pilots and considerably more experienced. Sneezy, also known on the squadron as Henry the Pole: "I was happy as lamb to be on Spitfire—superior to Me 109, in Tiger Squadron and, like tiger, to kill. I am very proud I was his Number Two on many, many occasions and defending his tail, because he told me to do and to follow blindly his orders. He was shooting down Jerries and I was very close to him, defending him. Order is order. Once he told by radio to turn Pipsqueak [identification signal] on. Of course, I could not hear him; my radio was always switched off. My English [then] was practically nil, so why bother to listen to it? So,

poor Operation Room at Biggin Hill intercepted our 74
Squadron as bandits 12 plus, with Hurricane squadron over
Kent. Then Sailor show me two fingers up, so I did also show
him my two fingers up. He laughed and laughed—after pan-
cake [landing].

"He introduced me to Winston Churchill, when he was
passing to Chartwell, near Westerham, Kent. At Biggin Hill,
at dispersal of B Flight, when we came to readiness. He
[Churchill] smiled and shook hands with me and asked in his
usual deep voice, 'Henry the Pole, how many today?' I replied
shyly, 'Only one Me 109, Sir.' He said, 'Good. Many more to
come.' Then, in my broken pidgin English, standing at attention and saluting in Polish way, two fingers closed together,
said, 'Sir, please remember Poland was, is and will forever
be the bastion and the wall of Christianity of Western
Europe, so make her great, free and independent.' My flight
commander, Mungo Park, translated to Mr Churchill in perfect English. Churchill smiled at me again, puffed on his long
cigar, shook hands with me once more and bubbled, 'We will
see on Victory day,' he showed me his V sign and drove off.

When Henry was transferred to command one of the Polish
squadrons: "Sailor did not want me to leave, and fought like
tiger to keep me in his squadron, offering me B Flight commander because my English was improving rapidly, but no
luck. I had to go. Later, Sailor wrote about me, 'Henry the
Pole—pilot second to none.' Motto of our Tiger Squadron was
I FEAR NO MAN, but I did also add 'ONLY GOD AND
WOMEN.' "

August 11th 1940. Sailor: "I was Dysoe Leader ordered to
intercept enemy fighters approaching Dover. I climbed on a
north-easterly course to 24,000 feet and did a sweep to the
right, approaching Dover from the sea. I saw a number of
small groups of Me 109s in mid-Channel at about 24,000

feet, and as we approached, most of them dived towards the French coast.

"I intercepted two Me109s and dived on their tails with Red Section. I delivered two two-second bursts at 150 yards, but as I was overshooting I went off and the remainder of the section continued the attack. I immediately climbed back towards where Blue and Green Sections were waiting above and tried to attract their attention, but due to R/T difficulties did not manage to get them to form up on me.

"I proceeded towards Dover by myself. I attacked two Me109s at 25,000 feet about mid-Channel, delivered two two-second bursts with deflection at the rearmost one and saw my bullets entering the fuselage with about 15 degrees deflection. He immediately flicked off to the left, and I delivered two long bursts at the leading one. He poured out quite a quantity of white vapor. Eight Me109s, who had previously escaped my attention, dived towards me, and I climbed in a right-hand spiral and they made no attempt to follow. I proceeded towards Dover on the climb and saw ten Me109s at 27,000 feet in line astern with one straggler, which I tried to pick off, but was unable to close the range without being turned on to by the leader of the formation. I circled on a wide sweep with them for about ten minutes whilst I attempted to notify the remainder of the squadron by R/T. This proved impossible owing to the heavy atmospherics, and in the end I gave up and returned to Manston. "N.B.—It seems that at 27,000 feet I had no superior speed or manoeuvrability over the Me109. This is merely an impression, and is not necessarily a reliable statement.

— (signed) A.G. Malan, Squadron Leader, Commanding No. 74 Squadron

On August 11th, three days after Sailor assumed command of the squadron, they took off at 7 am to intercept an enemy raid approaching Dover. It would be the first of four separate air battles they would fight that day. When the weary, sweaty pilots finally returned to base after their fourth fight of the day, they had downed an amazing total of thirty-eight enemy planes. The day was thereafter known as "Sailor's August Eleventh."

Malan led three missions that day, claiming two Bf109s destroyed and two severely damaged. Officially, the thirty-year-old was too old to be a squadron commander. But lead he did.

They were sent up three, four, even five time a day at the height of the Battle of Britain, to intercept and engage the German Air Force as its elements flew to attack targets in England. To say that the pilots of Tiger Squadron were busy would grossly understate the fact. The constant operation at peak performance left most of them near exhaustion physically and emotionally, but the enemy kept up the assault and had to be dealt with. There was little time in the daylight hours for even the necessities of life much less any indulgences. It was only in the rarest of moments that Sailor was able to dash off a few quick lines to his wife in Ruislip where she lived with their baby . . . until the Germans blew the roof off their house and they had to move to Norfolk.

Directive of July 16th 1940, by Adolf Hitler: "Since England, in spite of her militarily hopeless situation, shows no sign of coming to terms, I have decided to prepare a landing operation against England, and, if necessary, to carry it out . . . preparations for the entire operation must be completed by mid-August."

74 Squadron had begun building a reputation and tradition in the First World War and its WW2 pilots were anxious to add their achievements to the record. The squadron's most famous

ace was Edward 'Mick' Mannock. Mannock was the son of an army corporal, a drunkard who, on returning from the Boer War, deserted the family. The boy struggled through poverty and a limited education, but with the coming of the world war, he joined the army and managed to achieve the rank of 2nd Lieutenant. He transferred to the Royal Flying Corps in August 1916 and discovered his natural aptitude for flying. In France his fellow pilots in No 40 Squadron disliked him and resented his opinions about politics, the planes they were flying, and the conduct of the war. He had initially been judged cowardly by others in the squadron when he admittedly was very frightened. Within three months, however, his achievements in the air had earned him the Military Cross and he was appointed a flight commander.

Mannock had conquered his fears and worked tirelessly to perfect his gunnery. He described one of his victories: "I was only ten yards away from him, on top so I couldn't miss. A beautifully coloured insect he was—red, blue, green and yellow. I let him have sixty rounds, so there wasn't much left of him." By February 1918, he was "tour-expired" and had a total of twenty-three enemy aircraft to his credit when he was made flight commander of the newly-formed No 74 Squadron. Within three months his kill total was fifty-nine. Renowned for his impassioned hatred of the German enemy, he was remembered for remarks like: "I sent one of them to Hell in flames today. I wish Kaiser Bill could have seen him sizzle," and, on an occasion when he had forced a German two-seater to crash-land, and then machine-gunned the crew: "The swines are better dead—no prisoners." One of his fellow pilots said of it: "A really remarkable exhibition of cruel, calculated Hun-strafing." Mannock: "The other fellows all laugh at me for carrying a revolver. They think I'm going to shoot down a machine with it, but they're wrong. The reason I bought it was to finish myself as soon as I see the first signs of flames. They'll never burn me."

In July Mick Mannock began his third tour of duty, this time as C.O. of No 85 Squadron. On July 26th he shot an enemy aircraft out of the sky. Accompanied by another pilot, Lt. D.C. Inglis, he went down to look over the crash site and his fighter was struck by German ground fire. His engine caught fire and the aircraft crashed. Inglis: "Falling in behind Mick, we made a couple of circles around the burning wreck and then made for home. I saw Mick start to kick his rudder, then I saw a flame come out of his machine; it grew bigger and bigger. Mick was no longer kicking his rudder. His nose dropped slightly and he went into a slow right-hand turn, and hit the ground in a burst of flame. I circled at about twenty feet but could not see him, and as things were getting hot, made for home and managed to reach our outposts with a punctured fuel tank. Poor Mick . . . the bloody bastards had shot my Major down in flames."

Mannock was posthumously awarded the Victoria Cross for "an outstanding example of fearless courage, remarkable skill, devotion to duty and self-sacrifice which has never been surpassed." The VC and his other medals were given to his father, though he had stipulated in his will that his father should receive nothing from his estate. The medals were supposedly sold later for £5, but have since been recovered and are now displayed at the RAF Museum, Hendon.

Many years later, Mick's influence would extend to Sailor Malan. Mannock: "A sure sign of an old hand is that he reserves his ammunition and only fires in short bursts. If he is aiming straight he knows that a burst of twenty bullets is as good as a burst of two hundred and much more economical. Therefore, gentlemen, beware of the Hun who fires in short bursts."

Mannock's attitude was shared by another famous 74

Squadron pilot, Ira 'Taffy' Jones: "My habit of attacking Huns dangling from their parachutes led to many arguments in the Mess. Some officers, of the Eton and Sandhurst type, thought it was 'unsportsmanlike' to do it. Never having been to a public school, I was unhampered by such considerations of form. I just pointed out that there was a bloody war on, and that I intended to avenge my pals."

TEN COMMANDMENTS

The German air force had been assigned the task of knocking out the Royal Air Force, to pave the way for Operation Sea Lion, the Nazi invasion of the British Isles. In the first phase of the Battle of Britain, the Luftwaffe achieved little in the Stuka dive-bombing attacks on shipping in the English Channel and turned its attention to hitting the seaports and R.D.F. [radar] sites. The Germans suffered considerable losses in these new raids, but increased their attacking aircraft strength from 100 to 300 and then 400. With little to show for their effort, they switched objectives again at mid-month. Their aim this time was the destruction of RAF Fighter Command, its defending fighters and its vital airfields—Manston, Kenley, Dover, Hawkinge, Tangmere, Martlesham, and Biggin Hill. Though damaged, in some cases severely, these aerodromes were soon repaired and fully operational, and the great battle continued with renewed ferocity and intensified German bombing attacks, on British cities. The New Zealander, Keith Park, Commanding Officer, 11 Group, RAF Fighter Command, climbed into his Hurricane at dawn each day to inspect the damage to his airfields and personnel: "It was burning all down the river. It was a horrid sight. But I looked down and said: 'Thank God for that,' because I knew that the Nazis had switched their attack from the fighter stations, thinking they were knocked out. They weren't, but they were pretty groggy."

At one point in July, there was a lull in the air fighting and the WAAFs who guided their croupier rakes over the large plotting board in the operations room at Hornchurch had nothing to do but wait. Then, without warning, the calm ended and the loudspeakers on the station awoke. The word went out to ground personnel to quickly arm and fuel the Spitfires of 74 and the pilots, lounging in their deck chairs on the grass by the dispersal huts, were no longer as relaxed as they had been a few moments earlier. Under the brilliant, azure sky of that rare English summer, they too waited in anticipation, trepidation and excitement.

Ronald Adam, a controller at Hornchurch in 1940: "One of the most beautiful sights was to see against the evening sky the navigation lights of a homing squadron in tight formation. Round and round the aerodrome they would wheel, this twinkling cavalcade, the softer shade hiding the malevolence of their aspect, the dew falling, the flowers closing, and the deep rich hum from these flashing comets up above. The leader's voice would call, 'Red Section, break away, Go!' and section by section would peel off, until, floating out of the sky, the last three would touch down, and then cars and tenders would arrive and deposit outside the Mess their cargoes of tired pilots ready for their supper, their game of billiards or of cards, and deep sleep before 'readiness' once more as the last stars began to shine more wanly in the sky before dawn.

"It had a queer air of unreality, with battle far away and these lads dropping out of a peaceful sky with bullet holes and shell holes disrupting the extraordinary toughness of their aircraft, with their hair clogged and matted with the heat of their flying helmets, and still with a faraway look in their eyes of great distances and ever-present strain . . ."

By August 18th the Germans had suffered the loss of 488 planes, the majority of the crews being killed or captured, while the RAF lost 220 aircraft, with many of the pilots saved. There followed a five-day lull while the Germans regrouped before sending their bombers back to Britain, now in smaller numbers but with increased fighter protection.

It was on August 20th that the Prime Minister Winston Churchill made what would become perhaps his most famous speech, saying: "The gratitude of every home in our Empire, and indeed throughout the world, except in the abodes of the guilty, goes out to the British airmen, who, undaunted by odds, unwearied in their constant challenge and mortal danger, are turning the tide of world war by their prowess and by their devotion. Never in the field of human conflict was so much owed by so many to so few."

Prior to the height of the Battle, the fighter pilots of number 11 and 12 Groups, charged with the defence of London and the Midlands respectively, were given an important boost. Their early mark Spitfires and Hurricanes were converted from variable to constant speed propellers, raising their operating ceiling by 7,000 feet, reducing their take-off speed, increasing their rate of climb, and improving their manoevrability at high altitude. The change made them considerably more capable against the vaunted Messerschmitt 109 of the enemy.

The people of Kent and Middlesex counties were witnessing a previously unknown spectacle in the skies high over their fields, orchards and hop gardens, an elaborate white tracery of vapour trails, like chalk on a board, as the fighters of both air forces twisted, spun, and fell in hundreds of combat engagements.

Sailor: "How did we feel? Of course, we had our tails up. At that time the Luftwaffe seemed to be running on an endless belt—the fellow you knocked down yesterday seemed to be back next day asking for another wallop. We were not without fear. The fellow who wasn't didn't live long. We couldn't see behind us and the Hun was everywhere, ready to spit his guns.

"Yet fear and intense physical danger and the discomfort of battle were more than compensated by the very positive feelings nearly all of us had of satisfaction at being the only human beings who were able to stand between Hitler and world freedom. We knew that any day we might be shot down to death, but I will swear that this feeling of being the only spearhead, the only instrument between German domination and democracy was the one that kept us going and beat the Luftwaffe. It gave us all an elation that far transcended all else . . ."

One of the first changes Sailor made when he took command of 74 was the basic formation the squadron flew. Throughout his time in the RAF, the peacetime air force had flown set formations based on precedent and standing orders. In Fighter Command the basic element was a section of three aircraft, with four such sections comprising a standard twelve-man squadron in the air. The trouble with the three-man section was that the Numbers Two and Three were kept so busy concentrating on flying formation on their leader that they could not possibly keep a watchful eye out for enemy aircraft. Unless all eyes were free to scan the entire sky for the enemy, no one in the squadron was safe. As Bob Stanford Tuck, who had discussed the matter with Sailor put it: "I figured it out darn quick that the 109s were coming at us 'whoomph'—just like that, all in loose formations and we were flying all this jammed-in, odd numbers, which was absolutely hopeless. No freedom of action at all. You were concentrating because of the possibility of collision when you should be looking around at what was going on everywhere else. I eased them out into pairs when I took command. Copy-book formation stuff was hopeless."

While flying and fighting in Spain, the fighter pilots of the Luftwaffe had seen the wisdom of flying in two-man section elements and had continued to perfect such tactics in Poland and France. Sailor knew that three was wrong and two was right. He knew too, from the lessons of the First World War that the advantage of height in air combat was vitally important and by the time of the Dunkirk evacuation in May 1940 he had the Tigers of 74 Squadron meeting their German enemy at heights of 20,000 to 24,000 feet over and behind that part of the French coast, one reason why members of the British Army on the beach there frequently asked 'Where is the RAF?' They were there but were operating so high that they could not be seen or heard by those on the beaches. Malan influenced Stanford Tuck and Al Deere and the three of them steadily changed the RAF's accepted rules of air fighting.

It was when No 74 Squadron was posted for a short rest and training period to RAF Kirton-in-Lindsay, Lincolnshire, in mid-August 1940 that Sailor began developing his famous Ten of My Rules for Air Fighting, which he later refined while in command of the Central Gunnery School at RAF Sutton Bridge. His "rules" quickly became the classic tenets for the fighter pilots of the RAF and were pinned up in many fighter station crew rooms around England. Those pilots with the good sense to follow them often outlived their colleagues who ignored them. Sailor: "Generally speaking, tactics in air fighting are largely a matter of quick action and ordinary common sense flying. The easiest way to sum it up in a few words is, apart from keeping your eyes wide open and remaining fully alive and awake, it is very largely governed by the capabilities of your own aircraft in comparison with that flown by your opponent. For example, in the case of the Spitfire versus the Me109F, the former has superior manoeuvrability, whereas the latter has a faster rate of climb. The result is that the Spitfire can afford to 'mix it' when attacking, whereas the Me 109F, although it tends to retain the initiative because it can remain on top, cannot afford to press the attack home for long if the Spitfire goes into a turn. Obviously, there are a lot of factors involved which must govern your action in combat—such as the height at which you are flying, the type of operation in which you are engaged, the size of your formation, etc. There are, however, certain golden rules which should always be observed. Some are quite obvious whereas others require amplification.

1. Wait until you see the whites of his eyes. Fire short bursts of one or two seconds only when your sights are definitely 'ON.'

2. Whilst shooting think of nothing else, brace the whole of your body; have both hands on the stick; concentrate on your ring sight.

3. Always keep a sharp lookout. 'Keep your finger out.'

4. Height gives you the initiative.

5. Always turn and face the attack.

6. Make your decisions promptly. It is better to act quickly even though your tactics are not the best.

7. Never fly straight and level for more than thirty seconds in the combat area.

8. When diving to attack always leave a proportion of your formation above to act as a top guard.

9. INITIATIVE, AGGRESSION, AIR DISCIPLINE, and TEAM WORK are words that mean something in Air Fighting.

10. Go in quickly—punch hard—get out!

FINGER-FOUR

With the award of the Distinguished Service Order, Sailor's citation read "By his brilliant leadership, skill and determination he has contributed largely to the success of his squadron . . . he himself has shot down at least eighteen hostiles and possibly another six."

Sailor: "We are not so hard pushed now. Jerry had his tail up once. Now he's got it well down. We don't think he has a chance of putting it up again. We reckon that for each sortie we make each man should bring down four planes. That's our target. We don't do it, of course, but it's no use going for only one man and then coming home. Nor is it any use firing all your ammunition at one Jerry. Fighting is all teamwork. It's a good idea that we don't have ballyhooed aces now. All we want is to ground Jerry and that can't be done by individualists."

Rightly or wrongly, the great German ace Werner Mölders has been credited with pioneering the development of the *vierfinger* or "finger-four" fighter formation while flying with the Condor Legion during the Spanish Civil War in 1938. The formation was and is made up of four aircraft flying as two elements, lead and second. Looking down on it, the formation aircraft resemble the positions of the four fingertips of a human right hand. The flight leader occupies the front position and his wingman is to his left rear. The element leader is positioned to the right and rear of the flight leader, with his wingman to his right and rear.

The flight and element leaders are the attackers while the two wingmen provide protective cover for the leaders. Four such formations comprise a squadron formation, with each flight of four aircraft designated by a colour, i.e. "Yellow

Flight".

The Finnish Air Force is believed to have first employed the finger-four formation, in 1934, with the German Luftwaffe adopting it in Spain four years later. In Luftwaffe parlance, the two-pair flight was known as a *Schwarm* and each pair was called a *Rotte*. With ample separation, all four pilots are easily able to scan the sky in most directions for enemy aircraft without the highly demanding chore of maintaining close formation. The formation greatly enhanced each pilot's ability to maintain "situational awareness".

Critically important, situational awareness has been defined as appreciating all you need to know about what is going on around you—for a fighter pilot, the threats and intentions of enemy forces as well as the status of his own aircraft; understanding the state of his aircraft's systems and being able to anticipate changes and developments. It means having a mental picture of the location, flight conditions and intentions of your aircraft within a defined area and in relation to other aircraft and other factors affecting safety, including weather systems, terrain, obstructions, airspace infringement, loss of control, loss of separation, severe air turbulence, wake vortex turbulence, strong head winds and heavy icing conditions.

In the original Luftwaffe finger-four formation, the two *Rotten* could split up when necessary to operate as individual pairs. The *Rottenführer* or pair leader engaged the enemy aircraft while his wingman's role was to continue scanning for additional threats and to protect his leader. In the Finnish Air Force, whichever pilot spotted an enemy aircraft would become the leader of his pair or of the whole formation during the attack, as he had the best situational awareness of the flight in that moment.

Two aircraft being easier to operate as a unit than three, the finger-four is both safe and effective, with the pilots keeping sufficient separation and minimizing the chance of collision. The key to the success of the procedure is that it enables the leader to concentrate entirely on what is ahead, while the wingman's focus is on the rear and on any potential hostile aircraft which may be approaching from behind.

With the appearance of the Messerschmitt 109 fighter type in the 1930s, it was soon clear to the pilots of the German Air Force that the tactics employed during and since the First World War were no longer efficient or effective. The fast new, all-metal monoplane required a new combat technique.

Both the Luftwaffe and the Royal Air Force had long been using a basic formation of three aircraft that were flying in a V-formation known as a "Vic" by the British and a *Kette* by the Germans. In the brief peace of the '30s the popular flying displays led to much tighter formations. Then, when the Messerschmitt fighter was first committed to combat, escorting bomber formations in the Spanish Civil War, the fighter pilots experimented with flying in pairs. And, when Werner Mölders arrived in Spain, he is supposed to have taken two pair of 109s and created the finger-four *Schwarm*, with the second pair stepped up and behind the first and away from the sun. The advent of air-to-air radio communication made the looser formation of the finger-four possible.

The use of the new tactic, coupled with the exceptional flight characteristics of the 109, provided the Luftwaffe pilots the advantage they needed to prevail in the early air campaigns.

Some historians believe that the origin of the finger-four formation may go back much further than the Spanish Civil War—to the air war over France in 1915. The WW1 German ace Oswald Boelcke is said to have developed the concept of two Fokker E.1 fighters flying together and operating as a team, with the wingman flying slightly above and to the side to protect the leader from rear attacks. He is reputed to have flown the tactic together with his old friendly rival, Max Immelmann.

The finger-four proved highly effective for the Luftwaffe in the Battle of Britain and showed up the obsolescence of the three-aircraft Vic formation of the RAF, which soon adopted the finger-four against the Germans. Douglas Bader is credited with being the first RAF fighter leader to adopt the finger-four in his squadron. In the 1939-40 campaign against the Soviet Air Force, the Finns had a 16:1 kill ratio using the finger-four formation, while the Soviets were flying the conventional Vic but operating superior aircraft.

The Germans had thought of it as the Channel War, but to the British it had been the Battle of Britain and, effectively, the RAF had won it, ruining Nazi dreams of invading the British Isles. The young pilots of Fighter Command had secured air supremacy over Britain, obviating any attempt by the enemy to invade. Vitally, they had preserved England as a great aerodrome for the bombers and fighters of both the Royal Air Force and the American Eighth and Ninth Air Forces to operate from against German targets throughout the war. The end of 1940 brought the beginning of offensive operations for RAF Fighter Command. Now the priority of RAF Fighter Command was to "trail the coat", as Sailor put it—to fly over to France and provoke the fighters of the German Air Force to come up for combat.

Pragmatic, and with a no-nonsense approach to his main responsibility—destroying German aircraft, Malan was unimpressed by the standard formation flying of the RAF, which he thought nice to watch and good for drilling purposes, but not the answer in terms of tactics for the new generation of high performance fighters. He had studied the tactics and records of the great German aces of World War One— Boelcke, Immelmann, and von Richthofen. Sailor: "There was no false chivalry about the way Richthofen's Circus operated. Its attacks were concentrated, never diffused. Very often we sent up solitary recce planes—that was still considered a major job for the Air Force in the old days—and they were sitting pheasants to a concerted attack. Richthofen always picked out the lonely ones. He liked also to use his own formations as decoy ducks. He was very shy of attacking fighters near his own calibre."

Early in 1941, 74 Squadron, operating from Biggin Hill, had just scored its 127th kill. The squadron had downed the last thirty-three enemy aircraft without a loss of their own. Sailor's score at that point was twenty. In an interview of the time with the London *Daily Express*, Sailor responded when asked what it felt like when he was about to shoot down an enemy plane. "We don't have much time to think. A scrap lasts, at the outside, two minutes. When you are up there you're in another world. You see England, and bits of France stretching down below. You hear a roar and you know someone's gone down, or there are fireworks about. Knocking down the Hun is a foxy business. You've got to let 'em go sometimes, and get 'em the next day. The Hun won't always fight. He swoops down from a height, gives you a burst, and puts his nose down hard for home. He goes for stragglers. He won't join in a dogfight."

In five weeks the RAF pushed the enemy back about thirty miles. They used to be all over Kent. Now they were stopped over the coast. Their tactics seemed crazy to Sailor. Their Me 109s scampered over with a few light bombs and dropped them anywhere—mostly in the fields. Their fighters made their way across from France flying as high as they could, like lost sheep. "We would leave them alone for all the damage they did. But if we did, the artful devils might try to come down and machine-gun the ground."

With the coming of improved, higher performance fighter

aircraft, tactics were changing. Higher speeds and service ceilings meant that air combat was occurring at greater heights and putting greater strain on the pilots. The odds were changing too. The Germans no longer held an extreme numerical advantage over the RAF and, with their various commitments on other war fronts, no longer had sufficient aircraft resources to overwhelm the opposition in the west. The Messerschmitt 109 was still their principal air weapon and, with its six machine-guns and a cannon, was still a potent, formidable opponent to the eight-gunned Spitfire. But the Spitfire had a slight speed advantage over the 109, could make tighter turns, and its pilots had the advantage of being able to engage and disengage the enemy when they chose.

Influential RAF leaders were voicing strong views on the new tactics of the air war. Air Vice Marshal Keith Park favoured attacking the enemy bombers head-on, saying that the bombers' primary armament was to the rear. "Attack the ones in front. If you shoot them down, the formation will break up in confusion. Then you can take your pick." For the most part, he was right.

At an Uxbridge conference of operational air leaders the talk was of a developing Allied spring offensive. The top brass attending included Air Marshals Trafford Leigh-Mallory and Sholto Douglas. With the coming on stream of a new aircraft, the long-ranged Bristol Beaufighter, it was intended to patrol near the German airfields in France and engage the enemy raiders as they took off and as they returned from their missions. Leigh-Mallory addressed the gathering: "Gentlemen, we are now going over to the offensive. Stop licking your wounds. Last year our fighting was desperate. Now we're entitled to be cocky. Last year your morale was, shall we say, two points. Now it should be ten." But Sailor disagreed and said so. "You're trying to achieve the impossible, sir."

Like most in Fighter Command who had been flying and fighting at full throttle for more than a year, Sailor was near exhaustion and the strain of combat was showing, but he would not take a rest though he had been urged to do so by many friends and senior officers. He continued to lead the fighter sweeps into France, over the Pas de Calais, Picardy, and Normandy, in an effort to draw the pilots of the Luftwaffe up to battle, and as his own score of kills neared thirty, he was promoted to Wing Commander. Sholto Douglas, A-O-CinC, Fighter Command from October 1940: "It was a tough job as the Germans had a very powerful fighter force in the Pas de Calais at that time, and we were deliberately choosing to take them on on their own ground. Sailor Malan's tactical ability and advice were invaluable to his Group Commander, to Leigh-Mallory, and to myself in planning the tactics of these fighter sweeps. In fact I would say that, apart from his great courage, tactical ability and judgement were his outstanding characteristics. These, allied to a cheerful and charming personality made him perhaps the best of our fighter leaders in the early part of the war."

Sailor: "I was leading 609 Squadron with fourteen aircraft acting as cover for Kenley Escort Wing returning from Gravelines at 12,000 feet. We patrolled in three sections separated ten miles east of Deal at 14,000 feet. At 1800 hours, when turning through West towards North, two Me 109s appeared on port bow below and two on starboard bow turning to starboard. My R/T was unserviceable, and I dived to attack an Me 109 on port bow. My No. 2 attacked right hand E/A on port bow but blacked out as he pressed the trigger and the three Belgian officers unfortunately followed him and lost me. I continued and gave three bursts with slight deflection from 300 yards, and one three-second burst from dead astern in dive at 200 yards and E/A emitted heavy smoke.

"Three E/A on right turned towards me and I turned to starboard and evaded them. I then saw I was by myself and attempted to rejoin three Spitfires two miles to the West, but was attacked by four Me 109s and evaded them by spiralling and pulling up into the sun. Four Me 109s chased me on straight dive and were overhauling me rapidly at 9,000 feet in my Mark II Spitfire and I had to turn and spiral away. I had time to see what appeared to be a radiator on starboard side of fuselage creating the effect of a Spitfire end-on with the exception of wing section which was slightly deeper. I returned and landed at Biggin Hill at 1830 hours."

In another encounter a few days later and to the south of Boulogne, Sailor was flying a cannon-equipped Spitfire. He sighted about twenty Me 109s of a new type flying in a large V formation near Paris. He dived behind them and singled out the right-hand flank man, closing to fifty yards before opening up with his cannon. The German machine literally exploded in the air, and large pieces from the aircraft fell on to both Sailor's wings. Sailor narrowly missed the German's fuselage which was hurtling through the air. One piece wrapped itself round the Spitfire's feeder tube, which was fixed under the port wing and, when Sailor landed it was still attached. The Spitfire is an exceptionally strong machine and his plane suffered little more than superficial damage. All this took only a few seconds, and with his overtaking speed Sailor closed in on another 109, which was doing a right-hand climb into the sun. During his turn Sailor saw two more Messerschmitts spinning down in flames and knew the rest of the boys were doing their stuff.

He closed in to about fifty yards of the second machine and gave him a short burst of cannon fire. Most of the German's tail came off, and the number three of Sailor's formation said afterwards that the fin with the swastika narrowly missed his cockpit as it went hurtling through the air. The German went down in a steep dive at terrific speed and Sailor followed behind, not realizing that he was wasting ammunition on a dead machine. He broke off at 5,000 feet having used all his ammunition, and saw the wings tear away from his opponent's fuselage which plunged into the earth with a fiery explosion.

The press had fallen for Sailor in a big way. His impressive score of thirty-five aerial victories was frequently being compared with Douglas Bader, another famous Battle of Britain ace, whose own score of twenty got him plenty of acclaim. But neither of them seemed concerned with individual fame and glory. As historian Oliver Walker noted, "What distinguished them as pilots was a capacity for keeping in mind the complicated pattern of an air fight, and being able to explain, analyse and criticize it afterwards."

In his book *Nine Lives*, Alan Deere noted: "Sailor Malan was the first fighter leader to appreciate the advantage of basing squadron tactics on sections of four aircraft, spaced in such a way that each of the three sections, although an integral part of the squadron, had freedom of action in combat. The element of two, on which this formation was based, was a direct copy of the tactics so effectively employed by the German fighter formations whose leaders must be given full credit for their foresight in introducing the pair as the best fighting unit."

KEEP UP WITH ME

Most would agree that successful fighter pilots are a breed apart. For better or worse, they are equipped with qualities and characteristics that separate them from the pack, enabling them to excel in the strange art and science of hunting and killing in wartime. One historian has compared the born fighter pilot to a greyhound " . . . when he sees the enemy he goes for him, regardless of the odds." "Temperament, condition, and a good constitution certainly mattered," noted another writer, ". . . a pilot's fitness was not the same as a boxer's. A pilot worked on his nerves. His physical condition only had to be good enough for him not to think about it."

Sailor considered himself fortunate in his mixed parentage: "My father is descended from French Huguenot stock, freely mixed with Dutch blood, but my mother was English. The French are opportunists. The Dutch have vigour, tenacity, and patience. The English have more courage than any other people in the world."

Sailor believed that there are certain qualities a fighter pilot must have. In the first world war fighting in the air was, in his view, largely a matter of individual courage. Flying ability and good shooting helped, but usually the aces were men who waited until they got in close and who took terrific chances. It was different in the Second World War, he felt. Courage was a minor talent. No man was braver than the next. The civilian fighters in London—the air raid wardens in Coventry or Plymouth—these men did things under fire which the fighter pilots could only regard with awe. A fighter pilot didn't have to show that kind of courage. Unreasoning, unintelligent blind courage was, in fact, a tremendous handicap to him. He had to be cold when he was fighting. He fought with his head, not his heart. Sailor believed that there are three things a first class fighter pilot must have. First, he must have an aggressive nature. He must think in terms of offence rather than defence. He must at all times be the attacker. It is against the nature of a Spitfire to run away. Second, both his mind and body must be alert and both must react instinctively to any tactical situation. When fighting, there is no time to think. Third, he must have good eyes and 'clean hands and feet'. His hands and feet control his plane and they must be sensitive. He can't be ham-handed. When one's Spitfire is ambling along at 390 miles an hour, a too-heavy hand on the stick or a too-heavy foot on the rudder will send one into an inadvertent and embarrassing spin. One's hands, feet, mind, and instinct must function as well whether one is right side up or upside down.

Disciplined, aggressive, sensitive and clever, Sailor embodied the qualities he defined as essential in a successful fighter pilot. His stated opinion on courage aside, he was easily among the best of the bravest, most confident warriors developed in the Royal Air Force. He was well liked and attracted friendships, but was not sentimental and shied away from sentiment.

Sailor's capacity for living in the present greatly helped him to survive in combat. He did not allow himself to be overly influenced by his imagination. He knew his Spitfire intimately, became as one with it in the air and trusted it completely in combat. He worked hard to increase his ability to withstand the effects of g-forces, advancing from a point of four gs—the average black-out threshold—to more than five, where a target object takes on a grey even tone, eliminating the brighter colours which, at speed, are a distraction. He expected the same discipline in his pilots. In a spiral dive, acceleration and centrifugal force make a 180 lb man feel like he weighs over 1,200 pounds. Sailor would admonish his men, "I am setting my engine at 4-boost. If you can't keep up, go home."

Sailor differed in other ways from many of his fellow pilots. In addition to being older by five or more years than most of them, and more experienced of life and war, he was not one of the long-haired, week-end flier types; he had no particular interest in sports cars, and was never a habitual user of current air force jargon. Wholly focused and thoroughly professional, he knew where he was going and why, and stood out from the rest like the polished, tested air leader he was. He was utterly unlike the 'lost generation' types such as Richard Hillary, another pilot of the Battle and author of *The Last Enemy*, one of the great books to come out of the war. Sailor was one of what author Lovat Dickson referred to as "the tough, practised men who had come up the hard way, who, unlike the average Oxford undergraduate were not flying for aesthetic reasons, but because of an instinctive knowledge that this was the job for which they were most suited . . ."

After his rural South African upbringing and harsh merchant fleet cadet training, Sailor liked the 'democracy' he found in the air force, the fulfillment in the rank, seniority, and tradition. He had a special affinity for the people who did the real jobs, the pilots who flew the Spitfires and Hurricanes in deadly earnest, for whom killing in that situation was a profession. He appreciated their skill and deadliness. Aggressive, assertive, unemotional in the business of air fighting, like most in his line, he never saw any of the men he killed. Sometimes, when he shot a bomber down, he thought: 'Well, you won't drop those bombs on London tonight.' Years later, after the war had ended, Sailor remarked: "They called me a cold, ruthless, calculating killer.' "

The well known test pilot Neville Duke was posted to No 92 Squadron at Biggin Hill in April 1942. He flew with Sailor, who was then leader of the Biggin Hill Wing. Duke felt he was lucky to be serving with Malan, whose reputation he knew from the instructors at the Operational Training Unit he had come through, men who had flown with Sailor during the Battle of Britain.

The nineteen-year-old Duke had accumulated just 145 flying hours, only twenty-six of them on Spitfires, when he arrived on the squadron. At Biggin he served under Malan until September 1941, and later under Jamie Rankin when Rankin led the Biggin Hill Wing. While he was there the main work of the squadrons (92, 74 and 609) was fighter sweeps over northern France, close and top cover to bomber operations, withdrawal cover and rear support.

Bright, alert and capable, Duke settled in easily with 92 and by July was flying Number Two to Sailor on the frequent occasions when he led the squadron on ops. It had been drummed into Duke that he must, at all costs, stay with his leader—no matter what. Better not to come back at all than to lose the flight commander.

He knew that Sailor was a master at leading thirty-six aircraft in a formation, that he could keep station without struggling, had very sharp eyesight and would consistently report enemy aircraft and manoeuvre the wing into a favourable attack position before others had picked up the target. He knew too, that Sailor led the wing in a way that kept it least vulnerable to being 'bounced'—eg: keeping the sun in the right place to the formation as far as possible, not turning down sun, and having the squadrons stepped up or down sun as appropriate. Duke appreciated the great tactician that Sailor was, and how, during their bomber cover missions, for example, Sailor would not be drawn away by the enemy but might despatch a section, flight or squadron to deal with targets of opportunity. Sailor always endeavoured to give cover to such detached units. The squadron normally maintained R/T silence until enemy aircraft were spotted or until the squadron was in the target area. Sailor frequently provided a running commentary on the enemy aircraft situation and positions, along with forthright instructions to any squadron, flight or aircraft out of position in the formation. Flying Number Two to Sailor meant sticking to him like glue while at the same time weaving like mad and endlessly scanning above and behind.

On several occasions when dogfighting began, Duke was so preoccupied with maintaining position on his leader's tail and with looking around and behind for 109s, he did not know that he was on the tail of a Jerry himself. Once he suddenly found himself flying through bits of a 109 before even realizing that Sailor had fired his guns. He was showered with spent cartridge cases and links, which was awkward for they were known to pierce radiators, crack hoods and damage propellers. Sailor never flew straight and level for a second once they became separated from the main body of the squadron. He was a master in the air, and got everything out of his aircraft. With him it was full throttle work most of the time. From Sailor, Duke learned to weave and to search the sky continuously, never relaxing until they had landed back at base.

Duke remembered Sailor as "a very aggressive fighter, hard on his aeroplane (there was then only one place for the throttle—fully forward) with both hands on the control column. He was very strong as well, with a high 'G' threshold. It was a private dogfight for a Number Two to stay with him—he tore into the enemy and was always quick in attack. He was an incredible marksman and a 'snap' shooter, miserly with his ammunition and never firing out of range—it was really hard work staying with him, but very informative."

He recalled Sailor's meticulous ground briefings before and debriefings after a 'show', how his leader ensured that lessons were driven home during debriefings in a fair but pointed manner, and squadron, flight or section leaders (or individuals) seldom made the same mistake twice. It was good for them all and some lived longer for it. Those privileged to fly as Sailor's Number Two regarded it a great honour and learned so much so quickly. It stood them in good stead in later days.

Neville Duke remembered Sailor as a most human person with genuine concern for his junior pilots, but also with a certain ruthlessness—and little room for apparent emotion. He was relaxed and sociable off duty, but was not a great 'party' man. He was solid and reliable, and somewhat older in relative terms; a family man who lived out of the mess with his wife near Biggin. Duke recalled swimming parties at Sailor's house. He was very conscious of being a junior officer in those days, and Sailor a most formidable person.

Sailor recalled flying with one of his newer pilots, a good boy, educated and spirited, but, for some reason, never able to maintain his position in the flight. "He was a boy born to be killed. You knew or felt, that it was only a question of time before he was picked off. Yet the cruellest thing of all would have been to tell him to drop out of the flight, and recommend him for an O.T.U. (Operational Training Unit). He had lots of guts. He struggled hard to be a good pilot. But everything was against him. It wasn't just a matter of the aircraft he was flying, although youngsters are expected to take the older machines. He flew with me several times. I felt partly responsible for him. But you can't risk the striking force of the squadron for an individual. We were on a patrol one day with this boy flying No. 4 astern. Suddenly, looking round, he had gone. We never saw what happened. A Jerry must have sneaked up behind and picked him off."

Sailor had a lot to give to his young pilots and found them eager listeners whose respect and admiration for him was evident when he told them that, as the sole object of taking off in a British fighter on an operational sortie is to knock down one or more Huns, the ability to shoot accurately is a major requirement, and that a lot of tripe has been said about the cunning of the so-called expert fighter pilot. The more combat experience he had gained, the more Sailor was convinced that the chief qualities required in an expert fighter pilot are: 1. The ability to shoot; 2. Reasonable flying accuracy; 3. Quickness in reacting to any situation; and 4. Good eyes. Not everyone is naturally gifted in these ways. But a reasonable pilot, through diligent practice can make himself a good marksman. Having learnt to fly accurately, it's your business—if you are in the RAF—to make yourself proficient in applied flying. To a fighter pilot this means chiefly the ability to handle your aircraft like a gun platform.

He told them that whenever they went up they should take every opportunity of practising forms of attack, curves of pursuit, and aiming the machine at targets, both moving and stationary, to practise throwing it into quick turns on to clouds or any moving target within reason. They would also find that, by constantly whipping the machine into turns at high speed and half-rolling and pulling out, one will increase one's black-out threshold.

He said that the ability to react quickly is more instinct than applied. Some pilots are fortunate there. More often than not, the man who nips in quickly without a second's delay wins, because with the speed of a modern aircraft, a few seconds' start is a tremendous advantage.

Good eyesight, he told them, is also a gift, but eyes can be trained. The best training for a fighter pilot's eyes is to practise looking at distant objects. Whenever you've a spare moment at dispersal point, instead of gazing vacantly into space, or reading a book, spend as much time as possible looking at distant objects and spotting details.

Superior height, he said, always gives you the initiative, so always strive for it. Many pilots, who admit this, have deluded themselves that in combat other factors are just as important. One fallacy, for instance, is that if the aircraft is designed to give its best performance at a certain height, a pilot feels this is the best height to fly. He is thus throwing aside the essential fact that an enemy aircraft, with perhaps fifty mph less speed, can obtain the extra speed as well as the initiative by starting a fight from a few thousand feet higher with a diving attack.

He cautioned them to always cruise at high speed, and to train members of their formation to cope with a leader who is giving them the minimum amount of extra boost and revs to play with. It is better to cut down your radius of action and increase your performance. If the strategy demands that you operate at low cruising speeds and weak mixture in order to gain your objective, the strategy is faulty.

While a lot has been said about fighter formations, in Sailor's opinion, a fighter formation is only effective if it combines manoeuvrability, flexibility, and simplicity.

A fighter formation must never, never, dive to the attack without leaving at least one-third of its strength above as a top guard. This is a rule never to be departed from.

Strict air discipline, he reminded them, is essential for successful combat. It is good for teamwork and therefore morale. Team rules should be few and simple, but rigidly enforced. After each engagement a post mortem should be held. One definite rule he stressed is that the unit should fight in pairs. No. 2 should always remain with his leader, not as an attacker, but as a rear guard while the leader attacks. A junior officer acting as No. 2 can thus gain experience for the time when he is a leader.

He said that nearly all attacks begin to develop along a curved path of pursuit. This may not sound important, but it is vital. If the attacker is seen, it is generally important to avoid a stern chase, for obvious reasons. With a certain amount of practise the fighter pilot can soon learn when to commence his turn in to a target. In order to prevent a stern chase, the curve-in must be started from well before the beam, if the target is doing a reasonable speed. An attack can be delivered on a much faster aircraft provided the turn-in is started in plenty of time.

Once having closed the range, he continued, it can be decided whether to attack with deflection or to swing round to the dead-astern position. For the two main types of target, i.e. fighter and bomber, the problems are not at all similar. The bomber is most vulnerable from a head-on attack, and has its armour and armament astern and on both sides. The fighter, on the other hand, has its armour forward and aft and its armament generally forward. With the bomber, surprise is difficult, whereas with the fighter it is comparatively simple. It will be unprofitable to attack bombers from anywhere except from ahead and the flanks, particularly when they are flying in formation, which is their chief form of protection.

Sailor added that, when attacking bomber formations the best plan is to deliver the initial attack from ahead, provided strategy permits. After that, one should attempt to break up the formation if this has not already been achieved by the head-on attack. With the fighter, the head-on attack should be avoided at all costs and, if surprise can be achieved, attack with overtaking speed from below and dead astern, firing being withheld until extremely close. Resist the impulse to fire at any range except harmonized or closer ranges. Range estimation, although one of the fighter pilot's chief enemies, is the cause of most of the 'probables' and 'damaged', and is a very simple matter to overcome. Always aim at the top edge of the target.

Sailor felt that the German fighter pilot paid a lot of attention to tactics—a good fault, but unfortunately for Hitler, he seemed to lack initiative and 'guts.' His fighting was stereotyped, and he was easily bluffed. Part of his reluctance to stay around and mix it was due to his aircraft being less manoeuvrable. The German pilot insisted on using the same old tricks, without any imagination. For instance, he would detach a pair of decoys that dived in front of a British formation, hoping someone would be fool enough to follow them, and the others could then do a surprise bounce on the rest of the Brits. Despite many warnings, some of our pilots, have been caught by this.

He told them that the old saying from the First World War, 'Beware of the Hun in the sun', is truer than ever because: 1. The Hun seldom attacks from any direction except the sun, 2. The modern machine, with its clean lines and good camouflage, is more difficult than ever to spot against the sun, and 3. Modern high speeds allow less time than ever to evade before your opponent has you in range. Never forget that the man who knocks you down in air combat is usually the one you don't see. If the enemy is in range, so are you.

Sailor carefully explained that a fighter pilot should approach the problem of teaching himself how to shoot and fly in exactly the same way as he would learn to use a shotgun. First, your shotgun instructor shows you a shotgun—the various parts of it, its trigger action and safety gadgets, so, your flying instructor shows you your aeroplane and explains the flying controls and knobs in the cockpit. You handle the shotgun and get familiar with it. The instructor shows you how to hold it, and use it, so that you can get used to the feel of it. You learn to fly and how to handle your aeroplane so that you can get your sights in the right place in the quickest possible time.

When you can handle the gun instinctively your instructor will tell you the ways and wiles of ducks, and how you can find them and approach them. So, you will learn the tactics of fighter operations and how to fight. Your Spitfire is nothing but a gun with a couple of wings and an engine to keep it in the air. Your job is to use it as a gun and fly it as a part of you with your attention outside of it, until you have something in your sights, when your whole concentration is along the sight and on the target.

"Unless you take a tremendous grip on yourself on operations", he warned, "you're certain to fire at twice the range you ought to. It feels easier to shoot when the range is great; the contrast between the size of the enemy aircraft, from the speck it was when you first saw it, to the size of it when you feel close enough to shoot, makes it look as if it is two hundred yards away when it is six hundred. Sheer determination alone will make you hold your fire. There are two ways of judging range. One is to learn by means of the range bars, or by knowing how much of the ring the target should fill at, say, three hundred yards—and never shooting when it is smaller. The other is to notice, at a particular range, how much detail of the aircraft you can see—the crosses, the oil streaks, the pilot's canopy—and never shoot when you see any less.

"Whatever kind of attack you're making, always bring your sight up to the target from behind it, and carry it through the target along its line of flight until you reach the correct deflection; then fire. Don't hold the sight ahead and wait for the target to meet it. Otherwise, it is impossible to hold a steady aim without skidding and making the shooting phenomenally difficult for yourself. This is infinitely more the case with an aeroplane than it is with a shotgun, because an aeroplane is slower to handle and you are firing a continuous burst. Even with a shotgun you must always swing through from behind . . ."

World War One fighter pilots started the practise of favouring certain types of ammunition and having it arranged in a particular belted sequence. In World War Two, RAF fighter pilots were greatly impressed by the new De Wilde incendiary bullets (named after the Belgian who invented them). But early supply shortages meant that a mix of ammunition types had to be employed initially in the eight guns of the Spitfires and Hurricanes. Commonly, the mix was four guns with conventional bullets, two with armour-piercing and two with De Wilde incendiaries.

Sailor and Al Deere shared the view that the combination of "point harmonization" of their guns, and the use of De Wilde Mk VI incendiary ammunition, made the difference between destroying the enemy aircraft and only damaging it. De Wilde bullets were first issued in the RAF in June 1940 and had been tested operationally in air combat over Dunkirk. They proved far more effective than prior incendiary ammunition and were greatly appreciated by pilots, as the flash made on impact by the De Wilde bullets showed them that their shooting was on target. Al Deere: "It was most satisfying to find that my aim was good. De Wilde bursting on the wings was proof of this. Undoubtedly it was a big improvement; one supplemented the other and our kill rate was bound to go up accordingly."

A portrait of Sailor by Cuthbert
Orde drawn a few months after
the Battle of Britain ended;
overleaf: Pilot's view from the
cockpit of a Spitfire.

top: Group Captain Douglas Bader at his Duxford base; above: Friend of Malan and fellow merchant sailor, Wing Commander Bob Stanford Tuck in his fighter.

above: A Messerschmitt Bf 109 fighter shot down over England during the Battle of Britain.

above: Spitfire production at the Vickers Castle Bromwich factory in Birmingham.

below: A Royal Air Force sergeant pilot in the cockpit of his Spitfire in the late summer of 1940.

above: Air Chief Marshal Sir Hugh Dowding, Commander-in-Chief, RAF Fighter
Command, during the Battle of Britain.

top: The Heinkel He 111 bomber, mainstay of the Luftwaffe bombing force in 1940; above: the cockpit crew of an He 111 during a raid on a British target.

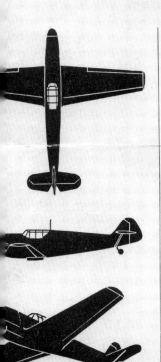

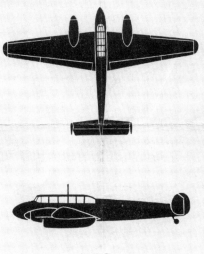

ERSCHMITT ME. 109

ny began the war with
hter. It is at once to be
ised by the square-cut
In side view the ME. 109
bles the Spitfire; but fin
idder are more rounded.
g wheels fold outwards.

Span: 32 ft. 7 ins.
Length: 29 ft. 4 ins.

MESSERSCHMITT ME. 110

The ME. 110 began as a long
range escort fighter and now is
used also as a bomber, known as
the Jaguar. Wings are tapered
to rounded tips. The tail plane
and elevator are square-cut and
the twin fins and rudders
rounded.

Span: 55 ft.
Length: 35 ft.

HEINKEL HE. 11

This is Germany's latest fi
It replaces the unsatisf
HE. 112, and follows the n
single seat fighter formu
clean, streamlined form.
are tapered at the trailin
from the centre section.
on, the fin and rudder is d
tive, cut straight at the
Landing wheels fold in

Span: 30 ft. 10 ins.
Length: 26 ft. 10 in

above: A British wartime aircraft identification chart.

The control column and
spade grip handle with gun
button, recovered from the
crash site of an RAF Spitfire
during the Battle of Britain.

above: A still from the 1969 film *Battle of Britain*, showing Robert Shaw in the cockpit of a Spitfire in his role as Squadron Leader Skipper, loosely based on Sailor Malan.

above: Kath Preston, proprietor of the White Hart pub at Brasted near Biggin Hill, whose kindness and hospitality eased the strain of the pilots at Biggin in the Battle of Britain period and through the war years.

The Spitfire of Sergeant pilot Denis
Robinson of No 152 Squadron,
RAF, which crashed in a field near
Wareham on 8th August 1940 after
being shot down by a Bf 109.

below: RAF fighter pilots relaxing on their airfield between sorties in the warm summer of 1940.

above: RAF Fighter Command Spitfire pilots.

above: Group Captain A. G. Malan was station commander at RAF Biggin Hill.

BIGGIN HILL

In ten weeks of the Battle of Britain, six fighter squadrons had operated from RAF Biggin Hill, south of London in Kent. On Thursday, August 15th, the German Air Force launched an all-out assault to destroy the Royal Air Force at its key fighter stations. For the first time in the course of the Battle, the fighter controllers at 11 Group headquarters, Uxbridge, were utterly confused by an array of simultaneous raid threats and feints.

The Hurricanes of No 32 Squadron, led by Michael Crossley, were scrambled from Biggin to the Selsey Bill area to intercept a force of 300 enemy bombers in the late afternoon. A London *Daily Express* reporter witnessed the combat: "To see these fighters diving through great masses of enemy planes, to see them tear, one after the other, out of the sky and rise again to dive back, is the most heroic and inspiring thing I have ever seen in my life. There are no words to express their fury and their bravery." It was the fourth of five major raids on RAF targets that day.

The pilots of No 610 Squadron, the second unit then based at Biggin, were airborne in that early evening, having been scrambled by Uxbridge to meet the late raid southeast of Maidstone. They managed to break up and scatter one large force of the enemy bombers, but a second formation got through to attack its objective, Croydon airport.

Sunday, August 18th. People in the village of Biggin Hill were emerging from church as an air raid siren began to wail. The controllers in the Biggin operations room watched the progress of hostile aircraft across southeast England and both of Biggin's fighter squadrons were at 'top-line readiness' alert status. At Uxbridge, 11 Group was delaying any interception commands pending a more informed picture of the enemy intent. The German formation seemed to be heading towards

London. But it was Kenley's turn. Bombs were raining down on that key sector station only a few miles from Biggin. All but one of its hangars were destroyed in the attack, along with six Hurricanes. Damage to the runways and several buildings, including the operations room, was so severe that the ops room function had to be relocated to a butcher shop in Caterham. Ten minutes later, the Luftwaffe hit Croydon again. 11 Group Command at Uxbridge told Biggin's squadrons to 'hold fast.' Then West Malling was hit.

In the Ops Block at Biggin, controllers tracked the progress of a new force of fifty+ German bombers as it crossed over Tunbridge Wells, about twelve minutes flying time from Biggin. The chief controller phoned through to the two squadron dispersals and ordered them up. Twelve Hurricanes were quickly airborne, followed immediately by fifteen Spitfires. Group Captain Richard Grice got on the Tannoy loudspeaker to tell his station personnel that an attack on the base was probably imminent and to take cover.

As the bombs fell on the aerodrome, a lone Dornier 215 crossed low overhead, burst into flames and, trailing thick smoke, crashed on the far side of the field. Fighters from the Biggin squadrons tore into the enemy raiders 12,000 feet over the airfield and some of the fighter pilots could hear the faint sounds of the bombing over their R/T. Leaving the Hurricanes of 32 to deal with the bombers, the Spitfire pilots of 610 climbed at full boost to intercept the German escort fighters above 30,000 feet.

The bombing lasted only ten minutes. Some of the WAAFs stationed at Biggin distinguished themselves in the ensuing chaos. Sergeant Joan Mortimer, who had been in the station armoury when the alert was sounded for the raid, stayed at her telephone switchboard, relaying vital messages. Then, before the 'all-clear' sounded, she grabbed an armful of red warning flags and went out on the airfield to mark the many unexploded bombs that were sprawled all across the landing ground. She continued to mark them even after one had blown up near her. The returning Hurricanes and Spitfires were able to carefully weave their way through the craters and bomb hazards, thanks largely to Sergeant Mortimer. She was later awarded the Military Medal.

In the raid, Biggin received 500 bombs including ninety delayed action bombs. No aircraft were damaged on the ground as all were airborne to engage the attackers. Of its personnel, two were killed and three wounded. Everyone on the station got to work immediately filling in the hundreds of bomb craters.

The combats went on at a relatively constant pace until September 15th, when everything changed again. To many this day is considered another Trafalgar, a day on a par with Nelson's victory, when Britain, through its air force, showed the world that, though greatly outnumbered and without Allied assistance, it would not be invaded. 74 Squadron was operating from the airfield at Manston on the 15th and took off on their first patrol of the day at 7 a.m. They climbed rapidly to 20,000 feet and were directed by a controller to a point near Dover where they encountered eighteen Me 109s. In a brief and furious fight they shot eight of the enemy planes out of the sky. The second patrol of the day for the Tigers of 74 came at 11:45. Twelve miles east of Clacton they met forty Bf 110 twin-engined *Zerstoerer* (destroyer) heavy fighters approaching a British convoy. The 110s lacked agility and this major disadvantage was underscored as the RAF pilots promptly destroyed ten of the German planes and damaged a further six.

Shortly before 5 p.m. British radar contacts caused 74 Squadron to be scrambled to patrol Manston. An enemy raid of forty-five+ aircraft was heading for the Kentish airfield.

When the Spitfires were at 3,000 feet off Whitstable, and just under the cloud base, they came upon the German formation, Dornier Do 17s, sometimes referred to as "flying pencils", an aircraft proven effective when first operated with the Condor Legion during the Spanish Civil War. The Dorniers were in four sections flying line astern. Quickly, and without loss, the Tigers destroyed six of the enemy bombers and were credited with another seven probably destroyed.

One memorable event that followed was a request for Sailor to attend a lunch meeting at Chartwell, Churchill's home near Biggin Hill. Air Chief Marshal Sir Hugh Dowding, chief of Fighter Command, had been asked by the Prime Minister to come and "bring with him one of his able lieutenants who would talk freely." The only others present were Professor Frederick Lindemann, Churchill's scientific advisor, and a secretary. The topic that interested the PM that day was how to beat the German night bomber. Lindemann offered an idea for fixing a million-candlepower searchlight in the nose of a fighter, which would illuminate the enemy aircraft, enabling escorting RAF fighters to shoot the German plane down with a steady burst. Sailor said that he didn't think it would work; that the Russians had tried something very similar and failed, and that there was the German plane's rear gunner to contend with. Malan: "But most of the time I let the others talk. I just sat there gulping and sipping according to whether the Prime Minister looked my way or not."

With the end of the Battle of Britain in late October, the strategy of RAF Fighter Command became one of provoca-tion—to make the Germans come up and fight. In mid-October, No 74 Squadron was moved to Biggin Hill where it shared the field with Nos 66 and 92 Squadrons.

In that splendid hot summer of 1940 the pilots of 74

Squadron split their limited free time among a few select and favourite pubs—the Star and Garter, the Queen's Head, the Bull, the Flying Horse, the Golden Cross (between Manston and Canterbury), and especially, the White Hart at Brasted, a sort of unofficial headquarters for the fighter pilots of Biggin Hill, Kenley and other Battle of Britain stations. Sailor, Neville Duke, Bob Stanford Tuck, Bobby Oxspring, Richard Hillary and many more enjoyed the warm hospitality of land-lady Kath Preston. They were her boys. Sailor: "Sometimes the usual crowd would come in and perhaps they would be a bit subdued. Then you would realize that a face was missing and the best friend of the missing man was sitting alone in the corner, drinking." In situations like that Kath knew to say nothing. They didn't want to talk about the missing man. No other subjects were taboo, however, between Kath and her pilot customers.

In her mid-thirties, she was a woman of maturity and expe-rience to these very young men. They would take her into their confidence about their problems and their love lives. Kath was always there to listen as a trusted and respected friend. She was fun too. A joke, a kind word, a game of darts and a four-penny pint of mild beer on the house was her way of entering into the spirit of things. It could not have always been easy for her though. Her husband Teddy was away in the navy and she feared for his safety. In her own way she was serving her country by cheering "the Few." She con-tributed immeasurably to the morale of those pilots and was long remembered by them.

Doubtless there were other Kaths in the lives of the fight-er pilots, but none could surpass the warmth, affection and caring of Kath Preston.

Sailor, on the afternoon of October 17th 1940: "I was leading Dysoe Squadron from Biggin Hill and took off at 15.10 hours to intercept fighter raids approaching London. I climbed mostly on an up-sun course to 26,000 feet and flew towards A.A. bursts over the Thames Estuary.

"At approx. 15.30 hrs. we suddenly saw two yellow noses (109s) crossing our bows and surprised them from the sun.

"I gave the righthand one a two-second burst with quarter-deflection from 200 yards and closed to 150 yards astern, and delivered another two-second burst. I closed to 100 yards and delivered a four-second burst which appeared to damage elevator controls as his nose went vertically downwards very suddenly instead of the usual half-roll. My engine naturally stopped when I followed suit, but it picked up again and I closed to 150 yards on half-roll and gave another four-second burst.

"I found myself doing an aileron turn to keep direction and delivered another four-second burst. He then started to smoke, but I blacked-out completely and lost consciousness for a couple of seconds, and eventually pulled out at 9,000 feet above 10/10th cloud. My port guns failed to fire during the whole engagement."

Sailor was promoted to command the Biggin Hill Wing in May 1941, when the wing included Nos 92 and 609 Squadrons of Spitfires. They were now operating Spitfire Vs, a cannon-equipped variant and a considerable advance over the Mark IIs they had been flying. In June, he was ambushed by three Messerschmitt 109s, but the V and his superior flying skills got him out of the predicament and he was able to down one of his attackers and chase off the other two. His next meeting with the enemy proved more costly. Again he was up against three 109s. He managed to shoot down two of them, but cannon shells from the third holed his wings and one shell smashed into his cockpit, wounding him in the thigh and wrist. He was fortunate in escaping into some nearby cloud.

He then struggled to bring his badly mauled machine back to Biggin Hill where he had to belly-land it. His wounds, while painful, were not serious and he was released to fly again within a few days.

In June, Sailor downed nine Me 109s. By the end of the first week of July he had been credited with a total of thirty-two confirmed kills, the record for an RAF pilot and one that would stand for nearly three years. A part of the citation to the Bar of his Distinguished Service Order presented in July, mentioned his "cool judgement, exceptional determination and ability", and ended "His record and behaviour have earned for him the greatest admiration and devotion of his comrades in the Wing."

A special occasion for all those who had served at Biggin Hill, the official celebration of the 1,000th Hun downed, took place in early July . . . a ball at Grosvenor House, London. More than a thousand guests were invited and, among the many V.I.P.'s attending, were the Commanders-in-Chief of Fighter and Bomber Commands. The music was provided by three RAF bands and a cabaret by the Windmill Theatre Company. It was a memorable occasion for all those at Biggin Hill, both past and present, whether on the ground or in the air.

One of the things that made it special was an unexpected gesture from a group of London taxi-drivers, members of the Beaufort Club, who arrived en masse just before the party officially ended. The cabbies offered their services free of charge to the Biggin pilots and their guests. In the early hours of the morning some of the taxi drivers in the foyer were asking for 'Sailor'. They were elbowing their way through the departing guests, and at their head a cockney was exclaiming indignantly to an obstructing doorman: 'Ere, cock, we're the boys from the Beaufort Club, come to offer free taxis to 'Sailor' Malan.

This most generous offer was gladly accepted and, a week later 'Sailor' returned the favour when he invited fifty cabbies to be guests-of-honour at Biggin Hill. They arrived in a fleet of cabs, the leading one of which carried a grandfather clock strapped to the roof. The clock, together with a steering wheel suitably inscribed, were solemnly presented to the Mess by the cabbies as mementos of their visit, and both were proudly displayed in the Officers' Mess.

The cabbies' departure at a very late hour was quite a spectacle; a dozen taxis in line-astern formation, wove their way through the Mess gates in typical fighter pilot style. From that time onwards, Biggin pilots experienced no difficulty in obtaining a taxi in London—a ring to the Beaufort Club, whatever the hour, always met with an immediate response.

On another, earlier occasion, the 25th anniversary of the founding of the Royal Air Force, Sailor had addressed the officers, N.C.O.s, and other ranks at Biggin Hill: "You are members of the Sector Station which has produced the most outstanding achievements in the Battle of Britain and which, not being content with the standards set in 1940, has continued in the lead as the foremost sector in this Command.

"Today, as most of you know, the Biggin Hill Sector is very closely approaching its thousandth confirmed victory, not to mention the 'probably confirmed' and 'unconfirmed'.

"I would like to say a few words in recognition of the magnificent support the pilots have always received from the ground personnel, whether their duties have been concerned with the direct servicing of aircraft at dispersals, the dirty and arduous work in the workshops, whether they have been concerned with the supply of equipment for pilots and aircraft, or whether they have been concerned with their payment, their clothing, their cooking, or their living conditions.

You people who work in the background seldom get either official or public recognition. This is chiefly because your duties are not so glamorous and do not make 'front page' news.

"When you leave this parade today I want you to bear in mind that your duties, however boring and non-essential they may appear at times, are absolutely vital to the successful continuation and termination of this grim war. Whenever you feel bored, tired, or dispirited I would like you to remember this. I want you to realize that you are honoured by being allowed to serve in a fighting machine that has performed wonders in the past and is playing a major part in the war effort. Every minute of every day which you spend at your work, you are performing a task which is making history and which will go down to posterity as the most glorious achievement by a magnificent Service at a time when its country and Empire needed it most."

COMBAT REPORT

May 24th 1940. Sailor and eight other Spitfire pilots of No 74 were under fire from German anti-aircraft batteries down the French coast from Dunkirk. He received an R/T message that the enemy was bombing the Dunkirk area and he ordered the patrol split into three sections. He led the sections down to sea-level and up the coast. As they neared the Dunkirk beaches, they began climbing and soon spotted tight formations of German bombers with fighter escort, circling at about 20,000 feet and bombing the harbour docks.

Sailor: "I could not see the beginning or the end of them. The nine Spitfires were climbing at full power to attack the enemy aircraft." Freeborn was on Sailor's left, Aubert on his right, with Mould, Treacey, Mungo Park and the others close behind. They spread out as they approached the German bombers and were met head-on by the diving Me 109 escorts. Sailor opened fire on the nearest bomber, saw his bullets ripping into the target and watched briefly as it caught fire and, simultaneously felt the shock of his Spitfire taking a flak hit in the starboard wing. An instant later a bullet slammed into one of his flying boots and others cut his electrical leads.

In a steeply climbing turn to starboard, gun flashes registered in his peripheral vision from a 109 astern. He realized too that his ring reflector gunsight with its magic circle of orange light was no longer working, making his guns useless. He was under intense enemy attack and defenceless. He manoeuvred through climbing turns to evade his pursuers and as he climbed he remembered that he had a spare ring and bead gunsight on board the Spitfire. He got hold of it and managed to replace the unserviceable sight. But the effort took time and when he had accomplished the task, the battle had moved on to a different part of the sky.

Sailor: "I looked down and saw what I thought were three puffs from exploding ack-ack. Then I realized that they were three of the crew of the Heinkel I had destroyed, baling out. They were the first parachutes I'd ever seen open in the sky.

"It was a rough trip home. Bertie Aubert was killed. Johnny Freeborn was hit. Mungo-Park got one in the arm, and Paddy Treacey got it bad. At least his plane did. His engine was on fire, but he kept going till a bullet went through his windshield and he got a mouthful of glass. Then he baled out. On his way down a Messerschmitt kept circling and taking pot shots that peppered his chute and hastened his descent. As he got near the ground—it was just outside Dunkirk—French troops fired at him. He landed in a pigpen deep in mud. He didn't mind the mud. It helped to break his fall. He did mind the owner of the pen, a large boar which charged him and caused him to twist his ankle."

Treacey scrambled from the pen and rushed down the road before hiding in a clump of bushes when some troops approached. They turned out to be French and ordered him into the open where he managed to convince them that he was a British officer. They helped him get to the coast and aboard a destroyer bound for England. In a few days he was back on duty with the squadron.

Pilot Officer W. M. Skinner on Sailor: "He inspired his aircrews by his dynamic and forceful personality, and by the fact that he set a high standard in his flying. Weather never bothered him. He would frequently take off when the birds were grounded. On occasion, notably at Rochford, he would give a spontaneous display of aerobatics fully equal to the demonstrations of Supermarine's own great test pilots, which were acknowledged to be in a class of their own. Another example of Malan's supreme flying ability and powers of leadership was shown by the fact that when occasion presented itself at

Hornchurch or Manston he would take off and land the whole squadron in perfect formation. When it is realised that the twelve machines in vics of three occupied the whole width of the aerodrome, and the complicated cockpit drill allied to the high landing speed of the Spitfires, it will be appreciated that, to put it mildly, a very nice sense of judgement and timing was involved."

July 24th 1940. The A Flight of 74 Squadron was patrolling the Channel coast out of Manston and was detailed to intercept enemy raiders at 1724 hours near Dover. The flight sighted three Dornier Do 215 light bombers down near the surface of the sea. The Dorniers immediately turned towards France. While the Spitfires were still 2,000 yards from the Germans, the bombers began firing at the Spitfires to deter them. As the Spitfires closed to a range of 300 yards and opened fire and one of the Dorniers was observed to be seriously damaged.

July 28th 1940. On this day twelve aircraft of 74 Squadron were sent to intercept enemy aircraft above Dover at 1350 hours. The Spitfires went after the escorting German fighters, leaving the bombers to the Hurricanes. The Spitfires encountered approximately thirty-six Bf 109s at 18,000 feet above Dover, engaged them and pilots Kelly, Freeborn, Stevenson, Stephen, Gunn, and St John accounted for one 109 each, and Flight Lieutenant Malan was credited with three of the enemy fighters and one damaged. Pilot Officer Young was shot down and killed. Sergeant Tony Mould was shot down and baled out of his burning aircraft. He had suffered a leg wound and was taken to Dover Military Hospital. Pilot Officer St John suffered oxygen starvation and lost consciousness on the way back to base, but landed safely.

July 31st 1940. At 1529 hours, both A and B Flights of 74
Squadron climbed from Manston to patrol the area of the base
at 20,000 feet. Large numbers of enemy raiders had now been
plotted and B Flight sighted fifteen Bf 109s at 20,000 feet
when the Spitfires were still climbing at 18,000. The Germans
were approaching from port. The B Flight aircraft formed into
line astern while continuing to climb on the sun side of the
enemy aircraft. As the two forces closed, the Germans went
into two groups, six and nine planes, both in line astern. The
first group came after Blue Section and Blue Three, Sergeant
F.W. Eley, was shot down in flames. Another 109 attacked
Pilot Officer Gunn, while another German opened fire with
cannon on Flight Lieutenant Piers Kelly, hitting his port side
upper petrol tank and tearing the armour plating off. Kelly
recalled thinking: "How odd that this should be happening to
me over Folkstone where I was at prep school."

The holed fuel tank poured petrol into the cockpit, leaving
the him ankle deep in fuel. His instinct was to get out immediately, but he reasoned that, although his aircraft was damaged and he was soaked in petrol and being chased by two
enemy fighters, the Spitfire was still flyable and he elected to
stay with it and go after his two adversaries. The damage
made the Spitfire less controllable than normal and it slipped
into a spin. He recovered and positioned himself to shoot at
one of the Germans. He turned onto the second 109 but
immediately went into another spin. Recovering again, he was
the target of two more enemy fighters, one above and one
below. The aircraft below rolled and dove away, but the one
above hung back in the sun as if to attack. Kelly fired a short
burst at the first Messerschmitt, turned towards the second
and tried to get into an attacking position, but his damaged
Spitfire wasn't up to the demand and he decided to head as
quickly as possible to Hawkinge. On the way he found that
the Spitfire was handling well enough for him to continue

on back to Manston. Later that afternoon, the Vickers-Supermarine test pilot, Jeffrey Quill, inspected Kelly's damaged Spitfire and was pleased that the machine had continued to fly after receiving such serious damage.

In the other main action of the engagement, B Flight's Green Section was approached above by the second group of Messerschmitt fighters. The Spitfire pilots turned into the attack as they continued their climb to intercept. Two of the Germans dove past the Spitfires, which climbed on to 23,000 feet and then lost contact with the enemy aircraft. Sergeant Skinner (Green Three), however, had separated from the section in the climb and, five miles out to sea from Dover, encountered a spread vic of three 109s 5,000 below him. He dove to attack the middle aircraft from astern, fired and watched it descend in a shallow dive until it was lost from view. On that day, Sailor was awarded the Bar to his DFC.

August 11th 1940. Pilot Officer D.N.E. Stevenson was climbing towards an enemy fighter which suddenly dived away. Stevenson followed and gave him a two-second deflection burst. The enemy aircraft lurched slightly and went into a vertical dive. Stevenson stayed at 15,000 feet and saw the German dive straight into the sea fifteen miles southeast of Dover and disappear in a big splash. He then climbed to 23,000 feet up-sun and saw a formation of twelve Me 109s 2,000 feet beneath him, proceeding north of Dover. He intended to attach himself to the back of this formation from out of the sun. As he was diving for them, a large volume of cannon and machine-gun fire came from behind. Twelve Me 109s were diving at him from the sun and at least half of them were firing deflection shots at him. There was a popping noise and his control column became useless. He entered a vertical dive, accelerating rapidly and pulled the hood back. He got his head out of the cockpit and the slipstream yanked the rest of him out of the machine. His trouser leg and both shoes were torn off. He watched his Spitfire crash into the sea a mile off Deal. It took him twenty minutes to come down. He had drifted eleven miles out to sea.

One shroud line of his parachute did not come undone and he was dragged along by his left leg at ten miles an hour with his head under water. After nearly three minutes he was almost unconscious when the shroud line finally came undone. He got his breath back and started swimming. There was a heavy sea running and, after an hour and a half, a motor torpedo boat came looking for him. He fired his revolver at it and it went out of sight, but soon reappeared. He changed magazines and fired all his shots over the boat. The boat crew then spotted him and took him to Dover.

September 11th 1940. Operating from Duxford for the day, eight Spitfires of 74 Squadron took off at 1630 hours led by Sailor Malan. The eight formed the rear squadron of No 3 Wing which was led by No 19 Squadron. No 611 Squadron flew in the middle. The formation had been sent up to intercept enemy raiders over London at 20,000 feet. The fighters of 74 were assigned to attack the bombers while the other two squadrons went after the escorts. Malan's Spitfires intercepted a long box of Junkers Ju 88 bombers over the capital and he ordered a head-on attack. Before they could act, however, a force of what the pilots described in their combat reports as He 113s (but were most likely Me 109s) dove on them. Sailor brought the squadron around onto the enemy bombers before the descending German fighters could strike them, opening fire on the Ju 88s. The Spitfires were split up in the fight. Malan pulled up steeply while duelling with an enemy fighter, causing himself to black out briefly. Sailor eluded the pursuing fighter near Biggin Hill and returned to Duxford. All the members of 74 returned safely to base.

September 14th 1940. No 74 was in the air initially at 1000 hours over East Anglia. Both Blue and Yellow Sections were detailed against Messerschmitt Bf 110s, one of which was set alight but not seen to crash. Blue Leader, Squadron Leader Mungo-Park's Spitfire, was holed by the rear gunner of the stricken 110. Forty miles southeast of Yarmouth at 8,000 feet, Yellow Section attacked another Bf 110 without result. Pilot Officer B.V. Draper, Yellow Two, encountered a Ju 88, half-rolled on it, fired and blew its starboard engine off the wing. Due to the dense cloud cover in the area, he did not see it crash. In a similar incident at 1500 hours, Green Section located an enemy aircraft five miles north of Ipswich. They attacked it, sending it diving and trailing smoke into the cloud cover. Thirty minutes later, aircraft of Red Section found a Heinkel He 111 bomber near Lowestoft and chased it in and out of cloud. The bomber eventually escaped out to sea with one engine smoking.

October 1st 1940. Green Section of 74 Squadron was sent to patrol off Yarmouth. Green Leader, Pilot Officer H.M. Stephen, sighted a He 111 bomber after being airborne for an hour and ten minutes. The enemy plane was cruising at 12,000 feet; the Spitfires at 15,000 with the sun behind them. Stephen dove in a head-on attack. The 111 climbed into a stall turn and Stephen half-rolled onto the German's tail. Closing to fifty yards, he fired a six-second burst into the bomber and watched pieces fly off the fuselage and port engine. Now critically low on fuel, the Spitfires had to return to base.

October 20th 1940. Patrolling the Biggin Hill area, 74 Squadron, together with No 66 Squadron, encountered thirty Bf 109s climbing from the south through 29,000 feet over Maidstone. Mungo-Park lined up on one of the enemy fighters, fired and saw it spin down to 4,000 feet where its tail fell off.

Pilot Officer Stephen audaciously attacked four 109s, causing one to break up in the air and another to crash in a wood. Pilot Officer Draper received bullets in his radiator and was forced to crash-land, but not before shooting down one of the Messerschmitts. Sergeant T. P. Kirk engaged a 109 and shot large pieces off its wings and fuselage. Kirk was then attacked and shot down. In the action he was seriously wounded and died later.

April 6th 1941. Flying Officer R.L. Spurdle was flying Blue Two in line astern on Flight Lieutenant Bartley. They left Manston, where 74 was then based, at 1630 hours. They crossed the Belgian coast at 1645 hours near Gravelines and flying just below cloud level at 1,500-2,000 feet, headed in the direction of St. Omer. They crossed the aerodrome and saw no aircraft dispersed and no anti-aircraft fire. There was little traffic on the roads and visibility was very limited owing to the low cloud base. There was a little tracer coming from what appeared to be an ammunition dump (separated buildings with blast walls). They came on a Me 109 in a field. It appeared to have forced-landed so they came in low and machine-gunned it. Spurdle saw a big cloud of brown smoke go up after F/L Bartley had shot at it. Spurdle fired a few rounds but observed no further effects. They climbed up under the clouds again and shortly after, heading NW, were attacked by an enemy aircraft which they didn't see to identify by type. Spurdle received two cannon shell hits and four machine-gun bullets before gaining cover in the clouds and losing sight of F/L Bartley. Spurdle's Spitfire was shaking and control at low speeds was very poor. He tried to fly blind but his gyro instruments were upset, so after about three minutes circling in cloud he came down to 'get a horizon' and let the instruments settle down. He came out of the clouds and saw an Me 110 just in front and slightly to his left flying in the same direction at approximately 400 feet. He opened fire and the enemy plane turned left and crash-landed in a big field. His machine was now shaking heavily and he entered cloud and flew on course 280 making landfall at Dungeness. He landed at Manston at 1740 hours, his port aileron controls shot away and a cannon shell through a propeller blade.

June 23rd 1941. A mission was to be flown in the early evening escorting six Blenheim bombers of No 107 Squadron whose target was the airfield at Mardyck on the French coast. The Biggin Hill Wing took off at 7:47 p.m. with Sailor in the lead. They crossed into France at 8:20 p.m. at between 25,000 and 27,000 feet on a course towards St Omer. Sailor spotted a formation of up to twenty aircraft down around 20,000 feet flying in pairs. They appeared to be heading from Boulogne towards Hardelot. Sailor called on the R/T for the pilots of 74 and 92 Squadrons to follow him as he was about to turn to attack the formation that he now saw were Me 109s. Jamie Rankin, in the lead of 92 Squadron, heard Malan's order and followed him with the squadron, but the pilots of 74 did not hear the order.

Sailor turned, descending onto the tail of a Messerschmitt on the right of the enemy formation, firing both cannon and guns at a range of fifty yards. As he watched, the 109 became a fireball, spattering Sailor's Spitfire with fragments, oil and debris which caused damage to his port wing and starboard wingroot. As the enemy plane seemed about to disintegrate, a big section spun back and nearly struck the Spitfire. Sailor then saw another German fighter to his right and climbing up-sun. Again, he was able to tightly manoeuvre into position behind it and close to within fifty yards before applying a two-second burst of guns and cannon to the 109. The German was badly damaged and drifted into a half-roll before plunging into a final dive. Sailor cleared his tail to be sure no enemy aircraft was chasing him and he raced after the diving, smoking Messerschmitt and continued to fire into it as they dived, until his ammunition was exhausted. When they passed through 5,000 feet at 450 mph, the 109 disintegrated, shedding its wings. They were about ten miles southwest of Boulogne when Sailor saw the fuselage of his victim hit the ground. Both of his victories were witnessed and confirmed by Pilot Officer Dougall of 92 Squadron.

The pilots of 74 Squadron who flew operationally in the Battle of Britain were Pilot Officer W. Armstrong, Sergeant D.H. Ayers (killed later in the war), Flying Officer R.J.E. Boulding, Flight Lieutenant S. Brzezina (killed later in the war), Flight Sergeant F.P. Burnard, Pilot Officer P. Chesters (killed later in the war), Pilot Officer E.W.G. Churches (killed later in the war), Pilot Officer D.G. Gobden (killed in the Battle), Pilot Officer the Hon. D.H.T. Dowding, Pilot Officer B.V. Draper (killed later in the war), Sergeant F.W. Eley (killed during the Battle), Sergeant C.W. Francis, Flying Officer W.D.K. Franklin, Flight Lieutenant J.C. Freeborn, Sergeant L.E. Freese (killed later in the war), Sergeant J.N. Glendinning (killed later in the war), Pilot Officer H.R. Gunn (killed during the Battle), Pilot Officer D. Hastings (killed in an accident during the Battle), Sergeant C.G. Hilken, Pilot Officer J. Howard (killed later in the war), Flight Lieutenant D.P.D.G. Kelly. Sergeant T. P. Kirk (killed during the Battle), Flight Lieutenant A.G. Malan, Warrant Officer E. Mayne, Flight Lieutenant W.E.G. Measures, Sergeant N. Morrison (killed later in the war), Sergeant E.A. Mould (killed later in the war), Flying Officer J. C. Mungo Park (killed later in the war), Flying Officer W. H. Nelson (killed later in the war), Sergeant Parkes, Pilot Officer Peace, Pilot Officer A.L. Ricalton (killed during the Battle), Pilot Officer P. C. B. St John (killed during the Battle), Sergeant J.A. Scott (killed during the Battle), Sergeant W. M.

Skinner, Pilot Officer A.J. Smith, Pilot Officer D.N.E. Smith (killed during the Battle), Sergeant H. J. Soars, Pilot Officer R. L. Spurdle, Pilot Officer H.M. Stephen, Pilot Officer P. C. F. Stevenson (killed later in the war), Flying Officer H. Szczesny, Squadron Leader F. L. White, Pilot Officer J.H.R. Young (killed during the Battle).

FLYING SPRINGBOK

History professor Bill Nasson, of Stellenbosch University in South Africa, presented a lecture in 2008 on Sailor Malan. In it he mentioned a few odd experiences he has had that were evocative of the Battle of Britain. One was the surprising sight of a cannibalised Spitfire in a Cape Town wrecker's yard, Barnett's Crash, Smash and Flash. He spoke of his family memories as well as the protest activities of liberal white ex-servicemen who had been appalled by South Africa's apartheid turn in 1948, the most prominent of them being the South African Battle of Britain ace, A. G. Malan. The professor was intrigued that this outstanding war hero also seemed to be a decent, conscientious individual who had stuck his neck out in the cause of common rights and freedoms.

Professor Nasson next encountered Sailor when he saw the 1969 motion picture *Battle of Britain,* which featured a square-jawed, no-nonsense version of fighter pilot Malan, called 'Squadron Leader Skipper'. Confident, courageous, with no patience for flying fools, the part was played by the late English actor Robert Shaw. Shaw forcefully replicated the real-life Sailor Malan in the role, effectively portraying the commander of No 74 Squadron in August 1940, hard on himself, hard on his pilots.

Bill Nasson points to Sailor as the product of an Afrikaner-Anglo landed family with their French Huguenot ancestry: "the decent civilities of the Wellington Malans encompassed instinctive loyalty to the British Crown. In such affinities, the upbringing of A. G. Malan was a world away from that of Cape Malans of an Afrikaner stripe. The most prominent political fruit of their Riebeck Kasteel branch in the Swartland locality of the Western Cape was Daniel Francois Malan, [a distant relation and] South Africa's first National Party prime minister, who once described the 'enemy' as 'the non-white' and 'the Briton' ".

As Professor Nasson notes, Sailor's World War Two experiences, and especially the Battle of Britain, in which he had "helped to ensure the survival of the democratic European civilisation to which he felt so fiercely attached, an outcome which represented 'one of the key moral moments of the war', left its liberalising mark on him, as on a fair number of other white soldiering comrades of the Union's 1939-45 war effort." Like so many of them, Sailor had fought and longed for a more fair, inclusive society, "developing on the basis of some liberal softening of the segregationist racial order." He was saddened by the 1948 electoral victory of the National Party, and wrote to a former RAF pilot with whom he had flown in the war, that "South Africa was now in danger of 'losing its ticket' to remaining in the company of the civilised nations of our world, the 'humane' world of 'decent values' that had prevailed in 1945."

In 1951 Sailor joined with other war veterans in the Torch Commando, a combined project of the Springbok Legion, an anti-fascist ex-servicemen's organisation, and the War Veterans Action Committee. He became president of the Torch Commando, established, as he put it, to oppose the police state, abuse of power, censorship, racism, the removal of the Coloured vote, and other oppressive creeping fascism manifestations of the National Party regime. Among the membership of the Springbok Legion were a great many ex-servicemen who would later join the African National Congress under the leadership of Nelson Mandela.

At its height the Torch Commando had 250,000 members. They fought a battle with the Nationalist government of Dr Daniel Malan, who was alarmed at the number of judges, high-ranking military officers, lawyers and public servants that were joining the Torch organisation. Dr Malan passed a new law banning anyone in public service or the military from joining.

Professor Nasson refers to fighter boys like Sailor Malan and other colonial supermen like Al Deere as 'extraordinarily good for morale', emerging "from the anonymity of their squadrons to find themselves on the way to becoming national figures, faithful outer men of Empire who joined Britons in swarming into the core of national consciousness." He calls attention to the performance of Fighter Command, acting to instill a sense of self-belief and staying power in the British public, and to Sailor being prominent among those who were elevated from their squadron identities and shaped into individuals of celebrity, famous fighters, personalities who were snapped "sipping sherry with King George VI or waltzing around London ballrooms with actresses."

Nasson noted how press and radio correspondents were attracted to RAF Biggin Hill, south of London and near Mr Churchill's home. At Biggin they sang the praises of aces like Sailor and turned him into a 'legend'. Britain's finest 'Lads in the Air—They're out for the Kill—Up they go from Biggin Hill'. Nasson called Sailor a patriotic Afrikaner South African who had come over to risk all. Newspaper photographers and radio interviewers sought him out. The publicity treatment called for the fighter pilots to talk up their roles in the Battle of Britain and after in dogfight scenarios scripted by Ministry of Information hacks. Ironically, though, the professor reflected that while their fame for saving Britain grew, in a relative sense their military significance and importance was actually declining. From late 1940, the 'few' were gradually becoming the many. The previously critical pilot shortage had been overcome, and, thanks to Lord Beaverbrook, the aircraft supply was secure. "Heavy German daylight raids had virtually stopped. Having ensured its own survival and done its job against the Luftwaffe, Fighter Command assumed essentially a secondary role."

Professor Nasson addressed the phonomenon of the typical fighter pilot's casual vernacular and how to account for his cool detachment from a "draining drama of close-quarter destruction and death." " . . . a breezy treatment of deadly circumstances also had a serious intent: to lighten grim reality, to weaken the power of stomach-turning fear." As a commander, Sailor Malan was sensitive to the threat that fear posed to his pilots and how it could attack and damage the prime qualities of a good fighter pilot— "cold, unemotional intelligence, fierce relentless aggression, the adrenalin rush of the dogfight and the kill. If the pilot could not conquer fear, he was much more likely to get himself killed."

Nasson drew another comparison—that of Sailor to Captain James Bigglesworth, the Biggles character of writer W. E. Johns in the 1930s. In a similarity to Johns' flying hero of the Biggles stories, "he cultivated a terse and laconic manner in the best sports tradition of the English country gentleman". Combat missions were seen as Hun hunts, "at times there was some grudging respect for an audacious and elusive adversary, and German aircraft that were brought down made up a personal 'bag' or 'tally', as if 'the kill' were really a pheasant or grouse.

"For the enemy, death at the hands of the 'Springbok Spitfire Killer' was the death of a plane, its occupants as incidental as they were inaudible. In its aftermath, 'you knew Sailor would be rubbing his hands, a bloody hard and cold pilot. He just hated the Germans, always wanted to make a mess of them.' Even his pathological dislike of Germans could be tempered by a patronising pity for enemy airmen viewed as lacking in courage. Snorting at a German pilot who broke away from his formation during an attack and turned tail, Malan did not take up pursuit, surmising that 'he seemed more concerned with getting away than with helping his pals, so I concluded that he was either badly damaged or badly frightened or quite possibly both.'

"Ground down by exhaustion, fatigue, and the dispiriting loss of comrades, one bleak night in September 1940, he buckled. Overwhelmed by despondency, he later confessed to a fellow Biggin pilot, he locked himself away in his room and cried."

Nasson noted that overseas men like Sailor Malan seemed to have had a unity of purpose in enlisting in the RAF. European war was seductive, a magnet for certain independent, middle-class young men in various corners of Britain's imperial world, promising red hot action, the chance to be where danger was, and to do something there through their desire to fly. The more sobering attraction though, was something felt by the approximately three hundred New Zealanders, Australians, Canadians, South Africans and Rhodesians who flew in Fighter Command during the Battle of Britain—a clear, moral obligation to go to war in defence of the Mother Country. "It was the loyal voice of Adolph Malan on the BBC, a volunteer 'inspired by a sense of duty to serve Britain and to fight on to save it from being conquered by an uncivilised dictatorship'. Conscious of being on the brink of an unavoidable war, he took to the air essentially in order to ready himself to fight in it."

Bill Nasson asked for what had Sailor Malan been risking his life? In his view, radical anti-war Afrikaner nationalists in South Africa caricatured Sailor when they weren't ignoring him. They presented him as a deluded poodle in leather and goggles, a contemptible man squandering his time, helping a British war effort aimed at saving a detested imperialism.

In Britain, though, an image persisted of Sailor as a brilliant Spitfire pilot and fighter leader, an "Allied Adolph who had sprung from a divided white South African society that could not make up its mind squarely over where it ought to stand on the war issue. Instead of humming and hawing, he had had no hesitation in turning RAF blue and in committing himself to the defence of a great British Empire." Sailor's war was a commitment to the survival of a free European Britain, and to "the anti-Nazi struggle . . . moving the moral compass of an increasingly liberal and reform-minded officer class in the direction of . . . a more decent and more fair society after winning the war."

ON SCREEN

Just as he was in the actual Battle of Britain in the summer of 1940, Sailor Malan, or a character much like him, was one of the prominent personalities in the movie that reenacted that battle in the summer of 1968.

When the film star Robert Shaw arrived on location at North Weald RAF station in Essex to begin his work on the picture, it was immediately clear to director Guy Hamilton that he would be dealing with a self-confident, consumate professional. Shaw was known in the movie business for being outspoken and forceful in his views. As a casting choice to play the part of a character not unlike Malan, he was superb. To Hamilton, however, Shaw was a potential problem in the role—a professional who could upset the balance of the film, and he thought he would have to keep a hard eye and a firm rein on the actor.

Long before his part in the filming began, Shaw learned that the scripted character he was playing, based loosely on Malan, was to be a paternalistic type who was constantly favouring the pilots in the squadron he commanded, with fatherly attention and concern. Shaw did some research into Sailor and discovered that the real Malan had been quite different from the character in the screenplay. The real Sailor, Shaw stated in the book *The Battle of Britain The Making of a Film* by Leonard Mosley, "was ruthless and he was efficient. He had a black hatred for the Germans. He ran his own squadron like an efficient business, and he despised anyone who wasn't up to the job. He wasn't running a public school, he was in the business of killing Germans— and he was out for results." So, Shaw set about adjusting his portrayal to shore up the Sailor character and bring it away from the edge of sentimentality where it was poised.

In the planning of the production and screenplay it was decided that certain characters—actual key figures in the battle—would be referred to by name, while others would be given fictitious character names. While the actors playing Lord Dowding (Laurence Olivier) and Keith Park (Trevor Howard), for example, were called Dowding and Park in the film, Robert Shaw played the Sailor Malan part, but was called "Squadron Leader Skipper."

In one memorable scene emphasizing Malan's hatred of the enemy, the crew of a downed German bomber have been brought to his heavily bomb-damaged fighter airfield. He is angry and bitter at the loss of several of his men and three of his Spitfires. The field is temporarily unuseable and, as he arrives at the hangar where the German prisoners are being herded by an RAF non-comm, Skipper roars: *"Corporal, where are you taking those vultures?"*
RAF corporal: *"Officers to the Mess, NCOs to the guard room, Sir."*
Skipper: *"Like hell you are. They're responsible for all that. Get 'em to clear it up."*
Corporal: *"What about the officers, Sir?"*
Skipper: *"Give 'em a bloody shovel."*
Shaw's involvement and performance clearly underscored the relationship and connection of his character with the real Sailor Malan.

The film would be called *Battle of Britain*, and was, after all, to be a commercial venture as well as a historical epic. As such, the makers were determined to have an extraordinarily "bankable" cast for the sake of box-office receipts. The picture would feature Sir Laurence Olivier, Kenneth More, Trevor Howard, Robert Shaw, Kurt Jurgens, Sir Ralph Richardson, Michael Caine, Edward Fox, Ian McShane,

Susannah York, Christopher Plummer, and a number of excellent German actors. The filming was to take place at various locations in Spain and England, including the former RAF Duxford in Cambridgeshire, RAF North Weald in Essex, RAF Hawkinge in Kent, and the former operations room of No 11 Group, Fighter Command, at Uxbridge in Middlesex.

Early in the movie, Shaw, in the Malan role, and two of his pilots land and taxi their Hurricanes on a forward airfield in France just as the advancing German forces approach the area. He climbs down, strolls away from the plane and shouts at an NCO who at that moment is loudly regaling a group of mates with a tale of some sort. Skipper: *"Corporal, refuel them immediately!* NCO: *"Yes, sir."* The corporal then returns to his story-telling, at which point the irritated Squadron Leader Skipper yells, *"Corporal, I don't mean with your blood! And re-arm them!"*

Of the many Second World War motion pictures with scenes of aerial combat, *First of the Few, Eagle Squadron, Angels One Five, Fighter Squadron, Flying Tigers, Reach for the Sky, Midway, Pearl Harbor,* and others, only the 1968 film *Battle of Britain* has successfully conveyed the visual experiences of fighter and bomber air crew. Its makers utilised the best cinematic technology of the time to capture some of the best air action sequences ever filmed. Unlike most movies of the genre, *Battle of Britain* was shot in colour for the wide screen format. That meant sacrificing the ability to splice bits of black-and-white gun-camera and newsreel footage into the film, as has so often been done in war films. But, as history happens in colour, the makers of the film opted for the power and immediacy of full colour. This required the film's planners to design and execute all shots from scratch, and called

for the use of a large assemblage of many fully-functional—
and some partially-functional—wartime aircraft of both RAF
and Luftwaffe types, and it also required several full-size,
extremely accurate taxiable replica aircraft. All the effort,
time and expense involved in acquiring, preparing, operating
and photographing the planes had to result in a final forty
minutes of magnificent, entirely credible aerial combat
footage.

Skipper's squadron has returned from France to England
and, in the early days of the Battle, has been re-equipped
with Spitfires. It is now stationed at RAF North Weald. A
new pilot on the squadron is approaching the field to land
and Skipper, a ground controller, and the rest of the squadron
pilots, notice that the new man has neglected to lower his
landing gear. The ground controller fires a flare pistol to alert
Simon, the new pilot, who corrects the problem and returns to
land, albeit awkwardly. When Simon walks into the dispersal
crew room, he is met by Skipper, who tells him to keep his flying jacket on and asks him how many hours he has on
Spitfires. *"Ten and a half, sir,"* the pilot replies. *"Well, make
it eleven"*, mutters Skipper, grabbing his own jacket and
leading the way out to where two parked Spitfires wait,
"before Jerry has you for breakfast!" The other pilots are
lolling on an odd mix of chairs in the grass of the dispersal
hut as their CO and the novice rush past. The pilots begin
making clucking sounds and one says *"Spring chicken to
Shitehawk in one easy lesson."* In the air over the field,
Skipper calls Simon on the radio-telephone: *"I'll try to get on
your tail and I want you to take evasive action, understood?"*
Skipper banks away and soon reappears, from out of the sun,
making takka-takka-takka machine-gun noises over the R/T.
"Hello Rabbit Leader," replies Simon, *"I thought you might
come in from the sun."*

Skipper: *"Don't think! Don't just glance. Look!! Search for the bastards! And never fly in a straight line or you're a dead duck! Now let's try it again."*

In mid-August, Skipper's airfield comes under a German bombing attack and a squadron scramble is ordered. He runs from the dispersal hut towards his Spitfire and passes one of his pilots who is standing, holding a cup of tea and looking utterly bewildered. Skipper: *"Don't just stand there. Get one up!"*

The film begins with the end of the Battle of France in May 1940, with some RAF Hurricane pilots high-tailing it back to England from their front-line French airfield ahead of the German *Blitzkrieg*. Air Chief Marshal Hugh Dowding informs the Air Ministry that, in light of the imminent invasion of Britain by the Germans, the nation will need every available aircraft and pilot to defend it and no more fighters should be deployed to France. The German Foreign Minister brings new peace terms to the British ambassador in Geneva and is rebuffed by the Briton. *"We're not easily frightened. Also we know how hard it is for an army to cross the Channel. The Last little corporal to try it came a cropper. So don't threaten or dictate to us until you're marching up Whitehall! And even then we won't listen!"* The German points out that Britain is just playing for time and it is running out. British Prime Minister Churchill tells the nation that the Battle of France has ended and the Battle of Britain is about to begin.

The Germans know they must achieve air supremacy over Britain before attempting a sea-born invasion and the Luftwaffe campaign opens with its early Channel attacks. The Germans try to eliminate the British RDF (radar) capability by hitting the Chain Home sites along the Channel coast. They then switch to bombing attacks on the fighter stations of the British in an effort to destroy RAF Fighter Command on the ground. The young, shockingly inexperienced RAF Spitfire and Hurricane fighter pilots strike back and the long, deadly battle of attrition begins. Dowding's commanders are arguing over the relative merits of employing small fighter forces quickly or launching a 'big wing' of many fighters to intercept the enemy raids. *"We don't need a big wing or a small wing. We need pilots,"* he tells them. His resistance to using the new squadrons of mostly non-English-speaking Poles and Czechs crumbles under the urgent need for pilots to replace Fighter Command's losses. Unleashed, the foreign pilots perform brilliantly, inflicting heavy losses on the German Air Force, and are quickly made operational.

In early September, a German bomber force accidentally drops some of its bombs on London (forbidden by Hitler at that stage) and Churchill orders a retaliatory raid on Berlin. Furious, Hitler orders devastating attacks on the British capital and the Blitz is on. With the Luftwaffe bombers now concentrating their attacks on London, Fighter Command is given respite to repair its cratered and damaged airfields. With London the prime target for the enemy, the RAF can now direct a large force against the Luftwaffe, which is requiring its Me 109 fighter escorts to fly to the limits of their range, with very little time left for combat over the target area.

A magnificent air battle, the turning point of the entire campaign, takes place on September 15th with much of the action over London itself. Both sides suffer major losses, but, to Hitler and Luftwaffe chief Hermann Goering, it is clear that they have failed to eliminate the RAF air defence capability, the prerequisite for the Nazi invasion of Britain. Operation Sea Lion is cancelled and Britain is saved from the domination of the invaders. Crucially, the island is preserved as a base later in the war for the bombers of the RAF and the U.S. Eighth Air Force in their day and night combined strategic bombing campaign against Germany and German-occupied Europe.

At the height of the Battle, Skipper is leading his squadron up to intercept a large force of German raiders entering British airspace. He impatiently awaits vectoring information from "Cowslip", his ground controller: *"For Christ's sake, Cowslip, wake up, will you!"* *"Rabbit Leader, sorry about that. This is Cowslip."* Skipper: *"About time, too. Where'd they go?"* Cowslip: *"Bandits now twenty miles east of you, heading southeast. Steer one-two-zero and make angels two-zero."* Skipper: *"Come in Red Two. Where the hell are you? Where the hell are you, Simon?"* Simon is then shot down by a German fighter—from out of the sun. Skipper (to his pilots in the air as they sight the enemy formation): *"Rabbit Squadron, Tally-ho, Tally-ho. Red Section, we'll take the rear starboard. Yellow, you take the port."*

In the course of filming in England, a number of distinguished visitors and members of the press arrived at the Duxford location. On May 26th Lord Dowding, who had led RAF Fighter Command in the battle, came to the field. At that point he was confined to a wheelchair. Several veterans of the battle were present with him including Al Deere, James "Ginger" Lacey, Douglas Bader, Peter Townsend, Johnny Kent, Tom Gleave, and Sailor Malan's old friend, Robert Stanford Tuck. Before visiting the airfield, Lord Dowding had called at Pinewood Studios near London, to meet with Sir Laurence Olivier, who played Dowding in the movie.

Hamish Mahaddie, a former Stirling bomber pilot, served as chief technical advisor for the film and he thought it

essential that one or more RAF Battle of Britain fighter aces
be on the advisory team. He brought in Ginger Lacey and
Bob Stanford Tuck to fill that role. To represent the German
Air Force, the production company appointed General Adolf
Galland, who had been Luftwaffe General of the Fighter
Arm, and one of the highest-scoring and most accomplished
German fighter aces of the war.

September 15th—the major air battle of the campaign.
Skipper's squadron is about to engage a huge enemy force.
Skipper: *"Keep your eyes open for their escort."* Ground con-
troller "Arrow" to Skipper: *"Arrow to Rabbit Leader, vector
one-six-zero, bandits one-hundred plus, angels one-five.
Bandits one-hundred plus. Over."* Skipper: *"Rabbit to Arrow.
I can't see them."* Arrow: *"But they must be there."*
Skipper:*"Well, come up and look for yourself then. Nothing. I
repeat, nothing!"*

The movie premiered in London on Battle of Britain Day,
September 15th, 1969, at the Dominion Theatre, Tottenham
Court Road, and thereafter around the world. Reviews were
mixed. The opinion of many was that the picture was over-
long, did not come up to expectations, but did catch the
atmosphere of those summer days in 1940 and did deliver
gripping dogfights accompanied by truly stirring music.
Despite the criticism there seemed to be general agreement
that *Battle of Britain* was certainly among the best-made,
most authentic and visually pleasing war films ever.

THE BLITZ

Hitler's failure in the summer of 1940 to eliminate the Royal Air Force during the Battle of Britain, in preparation for the German invasion of the British Isles, led to his cancelling the invasion and redirecting the bombers of his air force to the destruction of London. He believed the bombing would demoralize the people of the British capital and force Britain to seek peace terms. In the late afternoon of September 7th 1940, he unleashed 348 bombers escorted by 617 fighters in the first of fifty-seven consecutive days of attacks on London by day and night. The raid continued until 4:30 the next morning.

Sailor's squadron, No 74, was active against enemy raiders on September 14th, mainly over East Anglia. At 1000 hours Blue Section was sent chasing a Bf 110. They caught up with it and sent it down in flames. Blue Leader Mungo-Park's aircraft received several hits from the bomber's rear gunner. The pilots of Yellow Section then found a Ju 88 some forty miles southeast of Yarmouth and one of them shot the bomber down. At 1530 hours, Red Section was sent to the Lowestoft area where they encountered a lone He 111 bomber which they chased in and out of cloud, finally sending it off seaward with one engine burning.

Sailor: "Many of us were tired. We had been pulled out for a second breather. Older sweats like Mungo-Park, Steve and Johnny Freeborn and I were using a few hours rest to train new pilots and snatch an odd half-pint of the local brew at Coltishall on the East Coast. Sharing our airfield was No 242, a Canadian squadron commanded by Douglas Bader. As far as I remember—I don't believe in diaries—it was a quiet day. Bader and I, and, for that matter, all the fellows in the squadrons at Coltishall, knew that Goering's nut had still to be cracked. The fact that at that moment the Luftwaffe was being assembled for its greatest bid only a hundred miles from us across the Channel, was unknown to us as we played our game of billiards, drank a glass of beer or lay on our bunks in the dispersal huts at readiness."

The bombing of London had entered its second week. Over the eight-month period of the Blitz, thousands of fires consumed much of the city. Many Londoners sought shelter from the raids by going down into the deep tunnels of the Underground tube stations. By May 11th Hitler had called off the bombing of London to concentrate the might of his air power against the Soviet Union, more than 43,000 British civilians had been killed in the raids with more than one million homes destroyed. In addition to London, several other key cities and industrial target areas were struck in the German attacks, including Aberdeen, Barrow-in-Furness, Belfast, Birkenhead, Birmingham, Brighton, Bristol, Cardiff, Clydebank, Coventry, Eastbourne, Exeter, Glasgow, Kingston-Upon-Hull, Liverpool, Manchester, Nottingham, Plymouth, Portsmouth, Sheffield, Southampton, and Swansea.

War correspondent Ernie Pyle observed the Second World War from many vantage points in Europe and the Pacific. He witnessed and described one of the night bombing raids of the London Blitz: "Some day when peace has returned to this odd world I want to come to London again and stand on a certain balcony on a moonlit night and look down upon the peaceful silver curve of the Thames with its dark bridges. And standing there, I want to tell somebody who has never seen it how London looked on a certain night in the holiday season of the year 1940. For on that night this old, old city was— even though I must bite my tongue in shame for saying it— the most beautiful sight I have ever seen. It was a night when

London was ringed and stabbed with fire.

"They came just after dark, and somehow you could sense from the quick, bitter firing of the guns that there was to be no monkey business this night.

"Shortly after the sirens wailed you could hear the Germans grinding overhead. In my room, with its black curtains drawn across the windows, you could feel the shake from the guns. You could hear the boom, crump, crump, crump, of heavy bombs at their work of tearing buildings apart. They were not too far away.

"Half an hour after the firing started I gathered a couple of friends and went to a high, darkened balcony that gave us a view of a third of the entire circle of London. As we stepped out onto the balcony a vast inner excitement came over all of us—an excitement that had neither fear nor horror in it, because it was too full of awe.

"You have all seen big fires, but I doubt if you have ever seen the whole horizon of a city lined with great fires— scores of them, perhaps hundreds. There was something inspiring just in the awful savagery of it.

"The closest fires were near enough for us to hear the crackling flames and the yells of firemen. Little fires grew into big ones even as we watched. Big ones died down under the firemen's valor, only to break out again later.

"About every two minutes a new wave of planes would be over. The motors seemed to grind rather than roar, and to have an angry pulsation, like a bee buzzing in blind fury.

"The guns did not make a constant overwhelming din as in those terrible days of September. They were intermittent— sometimes a few seconds apart, sometimes a minute or more. Their sound was sharp, near by; and soft and muddled, far away. They were everywhere over London.

"Into the dark shadowed spaces below us, while we watched, whole batches of incendiary bombs fell. We saw two dozen go off in two seconds. They flashed terrifically, then quickly simmered down to pin points of dazzling white, burning ferociously. These white pin points would go out one by one, as the unseen heroes of the moment smothered them with sand. But also, while we watched, other pin-points would burn on, and soon a yellow flame would leap up from the white center. They had done their work—another building was on fire.

"The greatest of all the fires was directly in front of us. Flames seemed to whip hundreds of feet into the air. Pinkish-white smoke ballooned upward in a great cloud, and out of this cloud there gradually took shape—so faintly at first that we weren't sure we saw correctly—the gigantic dome of St. Paul's Cathedral.

"St. Paul's was surrounded by fire, but it came through. It stood there in its enormous proportions—growing slowly clearer, the way objects take shape at dawn. It was like a picture of some miraculous figure that appears before peace-hungry soldiers on a battlefield.

"The streets below us were semi-illuminated from the glow. Immediately above the fires the sky was red and angry, and overhead, making a ceiling in the vast heavens, there was a cloud of smoke all in pink. Up in that pink shrouding there were tiny, brilliant specks of flashing light—anti-aircraft shells bursting. After the flash you could hear the sound.

"Up there, too, the barrage balloons were standing out as clearly as if it were daytime, but now they were pink instead of silver. And now and then through a hole in that pink shroud there twinkled incongruously a permanent, genuine star—the old-fashioned kind that has always been there.

"Below us the Thames grew lighter, and all around below were the shadows—the dark shadows of buildings and bridges that formed the base of this dreadful masterpiece.

"Later on I borrowed a tin hat and went out among the

fires. That was exciting too; but the thing I shall always remember above all the other things in my life is the monstrous loveliness of that one single view of London on a holiday night—London stabbed with great fires, shaken by explosions, its dark regions along the Thames sparkling with the pin-points of white-hot bombs, all of it roofed over with a ceiling of pink that held bursting shells, balloons, flares and the grind of vicious engines. And in yourself the excitement and anticipation and wonder in your soul that this could be happening at all.

"These things all went together to make the most hateful, most beautiful single scene I have ever known."

We used to say 'If pigs could fly!' / And now they do. / I saw one sailing in the sky / Some thousand feet above his sty, / A fat one, too! / I scarcely could believe my eyes, / So just imagine my surprise / To see so corpulent a pig Inconsequently dance a jig / upon a cloud. / And, when elated by the show / I clapped my hands and called 'Bravo!' He turned and bowed. / Then, all at once, he seemed to flop and dived behind a chimney-top / out of my sight. 'He's down thought I; but not at all, / 'Twas only pride that had the fall: To my delight / He rose, quite gay and debonair, Resolved to go on dancing there / Both day and night. / So pigs can fly, They really do, / This chap, though anchored in the slime, Could reach an altitude sublime—A pig, 'tis true! / I wish I knew / Just how not only pigs but men / Might rise to nobler heights again / Right in the blue / And start anew!
—May Morton

In 1941, the American President Franklin D. Roosevelt appointed John Gilbert Winant U.S. Ambassador to Great Britain. Winant was succeeding the pro-appeasement ambassador Joseph P. Kennedy, Sr. When Winant arrived at

Bristol Airport, England, in March 1941, he told the press: "I'm very glad to be here. There is no place I'd rather be at this time than in England." His remark made the front pages of all the major papers in Britain the next day. The country had just come through the Battle of Britain and was in the midst of the bombing Blitz on London. Winant: "It was a very changed country from the earlier days of the war. Everywhere the enemy bombing had left great gashes in the buildings of London, its suburbs, and in coastal towns. Anti- aircraft guns were placed at all strategic points, in streets, in parks, and in the countryside; and over London and southern towns hung a curtain of blimps to prevent low dive-bombing."

Winant noted that the pattern of civilian life had severely changed too. There had been a hardening of resolution and there was a sense of grim determination everywhere, which seemed to have intensified after the Fall of France and the heavy bombing which had begun that September. The German bombing had taken a massive toll of death, and left a strange existence for the British people. He recalled the people taking cover in the public shelters and in the subways, and the often overlooked majority of people still living in their own homes. In the larger homes people sheltered in a basement room or cellar, but in the smaller and less sturdy houses people adjusted their lives to stranger conditions. Many spent nights in their Anderson shelters—corrugated iron arches sunk deep into the earth and covered with soil. Thousands of people owed their lives to them. Entire families moved into them each night, and in the damp and dark atmosphere, often sharing them with their neighbours, spent an uneasy time trying to sleep amid the noise of dropping bombs and anti-aircraft bursts.

Later, in 1941, the Morrison shelter was introduced. Table-shaped and made of steel, with a heavy wire netting around the sides to protect the occupants against flying objects and falling ceilings, this house interior shelter protected families huddled underneath it during the evening hours. In the day the Morrison was used as a household table.

Throughout the period, local authorities were concerned that a direct hit by a bomb on the pumps which carried water through subterranean London would flood the deep shelters and subways. They refused access to these underground shelters until the masses demanded protection regardless of this risk, and forced entry. With no shortage of shelter space available to them, thousands of people in the more heavily-bombed areas chose to remain in their own homes and beds. Most city children, though, were evacuated to safer homes in the country.

Often the wife and children left and the man stayed on in town, living alone in his home or in some hostel. And after a full day's work, all able-bodied civilians did their duty as air-raid wardens, first-aid nurses, ambulance drivers or fire-watchers to put out incendiary bombs, several nights a week. City life went on without crippling disruption.

When Billy Brown goes out at night / He wears or carries something white / When Mrs Brown is in the black-out / She likes to wear her old white mac out. / And Sally Brown straps round her shoulder / A natty plain white knick-knack holder The reason why they wear this white / Is so they may be seen at night.

Billy Brown's Own Highway Code / For black-outs is 'Stay off the Road'. / He'll never step out and begin / To meet a bus that's pulling in. / He doesn't wave his torch at night But flags his bus with something white / He never jostles in a queue / But waits and takes his turn—do you?

In the late autumn the rains came, the pace of the German

raids on London was stepped up, and the Battle of Britain entered its final phase. Sailor and the pilots of Fighter Command were facing up to another enemy, one nearly as challenging as the Luftwaffe. They were plagued by a particular fatigue caused by the physical strain of air fighting at high altitudes day after day for several months, practically without respite. Typically, their squadrons were putting up twelve aircraft and averaging forty-five flying hours a day, up to as much as sixty hours. From *The Narrow Margin* by Derek Wood and Derek Dempster: "It was estimated in the summer of the Battle of Britain that every pilot kept in action for more than six months would be shot down because he was exhausted or stale, or even because he had lost the will to fight. In terms of flying hours the fighter pilot's life expectancy could be measured at 87. During that critical summer the average pilot rarely got more than twenty-four hours off in seven days, or seven days in a quarter—if he could be spared from constant availability, readiness and actual fighting."

Snap back the canopy / Pull out the oxygen tube, / Flick the harness pin / And slap out into the air / Clear of the machine. Did you ever dream when you were young / Of floating through the air, hung / Between the clouds and the gay / Beblossomed land? Did you ever stand and say, 'To sit and think and be alone / In the middle of the sky / Is my one most perfect wish'? / That was a fore-knowing; / You knew that some day / To satiate an inward crave / You must play with the wave / Of a cloud. And shout aloud In the clean air, The untouched-by-worldly-things-and-mean air, With exhilarated living. / You knew that you must float From the sun above the clouds / To the gloom beneath, from a world / Of rarefied splendour to one / Of cheapened dirt, close-knit / In its effort to encoumpass man / In death. So you can stay in the clouds, boy, / You can let your soul go onwards, / You have no ties on earth, / You could never have accomplished / Anything. Your ideas and ideals / Were too high. So you can stay / In the sky, boy, and have no fear. — David Bourne

War correspondent Quentin Reynolds: "The Polish aviators are the real glamour boys of England now. They are terrific fighters. A Polish squadron is stationed near Blackpool. The Poles are so popular with the girls in town that the poor RAF pilots don't have a chance. After a long spell of lonely celibacy one English pilot decided that it was time for drastic measures. He went into Blackpool and walked around until he found something really tasty. He went up to her, donned his most pathetic smile and said, 'I am Polish aviator. Please have drink with me. I am very lonely.'

"After a split second's hesitation the fair lady agreed. They had a drink and carefully maintaining his broken English the RAF lad felt that he was doing great. He told her of the heroic fights he had engaged in; he told her of the Messerschmitts that were strewn all over the Channel because of his prowess and she lapped it up.

" 'But it is all over', he said sadly. 'Tomorrow I fly to death. I have volunteered for a very dangerous job. I fly alone to Berlin. I will never return. But I do not care. It is for England which I luff. This is my last night of life. If only I could spend it with you.'

"She looked at him and her heart melted. After all she was a patriotic English girl and he wanted so little. She would give. She patted his hand and said, 'Come with me,' and feeling pretty heroic herself no doubt, she led him to her apartment. Everything was wonderful. They climbed into bed and she sank into his arms. So it went for a while until our hero, ecstatic, his cup of happiness overflowing, cried out in delight, 'Sweetheart, you are terrific, but wonderful, but marvelous . . .'

"He entirely forgot his Polish accent. She leaped up, white with anger, gave him a healthy slap and screamed, 'Get out of here you double-crossing RAF rat you.'

"And so once more love's young dream died. All for the loss of a Polish accent."

'Good show! he said, leaned his head back and laughed. They're wizard types! he said, and held his beer / Steadily, looked at it and gulped it down / Out of its jam-jar, took a cigarette / And blew a neat smoke ring into the air. / 'After this morning's prang I've got the twitch; / I thought I'd had it in that teased-out kite.' / His eyes were blue, and older than his face, / His single stripe had known a lonely war But all his talk and movements showed his age. / His whole life was the air and his machine, / He had no thought but of the latest 'mod', / His jargon was of aircraft or of beer. 'And what will you do afterwards?' I said, / Then saw his puzzled face, and caught my breath. / There was no afterwards for him, but death.

"The American war correspondent Edward R. Murrow made a series of radio broadcasts over a sixteen month period early in the Second World War. They were called *This is London* and were a record of what London thought and felt about a war that began as something remote and hardly real and gradually became the dominant reality of daily, and still more of night, life. He was under no instruction from the home office in New York except to find the news and report it. The only objection that can be offered to Murrow's technique of reporting is that when an air raid is on he has the habit of going up on the roof to see what is happening, or of driving around town in an open car to see what has been hit. This is a good way to get the news, but perhaps not the best

way to make sure that you will go on getting it."
—Elmer Davis, reporter, New York, February 1941

September 8th 1940. Ed Murrow: "Yesterday afternoon—it seems days ago now—I drove down to the East End of London, the East India Dock Road, Commercial Road, through Silvertown, down to the mouth of the Thames Estuary. It was a quiet and almost pleasant trip through those streets running between rows of working-class houses, with the cranes, the docks, the ships, and the oil tanks off on the right. We crossed the river and drove up on a little plateau, which gave us a view from the mouth of the Thames to London. And then an air-raid siren, called 'Weeping Willie' by the men who tend it, began its uneven screaming. Down on the coast the white puffballs of antiaircraft fire began to appear against London. They were high and not very numerous.

The Hurricanes and Spitfires were already in the air, climbing for altitude above the near-by airdrome. The fight moved inland and out of sight. Things were relatively quiet for about half an hour. Then the British fighters returned, And five minutes later the German bombers, flying in V-formation, began pouring in. The antiaircraft fire was good. Sometimes it seemed to burst right on the nose of the leading machine, but still they came on. On the airdrome, ground crews swarmed over those British fighters, fitting ammunition belts and pouring in gasoline. As soon as one fighter was ready, it took the air, and there was no waiting for flight leaders or formation. The Germans were already coming back, down the river, heading for France.

"Up toward London we could see billows of smoke fanning out above the river, and over our heads the British fighters, climbing almost straight up, trying to intercept the bombers before they got away. It went on for two hours and then the 'all-clear.'

"We went down to a nearby pub for dinner. Children were already organizing a hunt for shrapnel. Under some bushes beside the road there was a baker's cart. Two boys, still sobbing, were trying to get a quivering bay mare back between the shafts. The lady who ran the pub told us that these raids were bad for the chickens, the dogs, and the horses. A toothless old man of nearly seventy came in and asked for a pint of mild and bitters, confided that he had always, all his life, gone to bed at eight o'clock and found now that three pints of beer made him drowsy-like so he could sleep through any raid.

"Before eight, the siren sounded again. We went back to a haystack near the airdrome. The fires up the river had turned the moon blood red. The smoke had drifted down till it formed a canopy over the Thames; the guns were working all around us, the bursts looking like fireflies in a southern summer night. The Germans were sending in two or three planes at a time, sometimes only one, in relays. They would pass overhead. The guns and lights would follow them, and in about five minutes we could hear the hollow grunt of the bombs. Huge pear-shaped bursts of flame would rise up into the smoke and disappear. The world was upside down.

"It was like a shuttle service, the way the German planes came up the Thames, the fires acting as a flare path. Often they were above the smoke. The searchlights bored into that black roof, but couldn't penetrate it. They looked like long pillars supporting a black canopy. Suddenly all the lights dashed off and a blackness fell right to the ground. It grew cold. We covered ourselves with hay. The shrapnel clicked as it hit the concrete road near by, and still the German bombers came.

"Early this morning we went to a hotel. The gunfire rattled the windows. Shortly before noon we rang for coffee. A pale, red-eyed chambermaid brought it and said, 'I hope you slept well, sirs.'

"This afternoon we drove back to the East End of London. It was like an obstacle race—two blocks to the right, then left for four blocks, then straight on for a few blocks, and right again . . . a few dirty-faced, tow-headed children standing on a corner, holding their thumbs up, the sign of the men who came back from Dunkerque . . . three red busses drawn up in a line waiting to take the homeless away . . . men with white scarfs around their necks instead of collars and ties, leading dull-eyed, empty-faced women across to the busses.

"Most of them carried little cheap cardboard suitcases and sometimes bulging paper shopping bags. That was all they had left. There was still fire and smoke along the river, but the fire fighters and the demolition squads have done their work well."

Into the paddock from his parachute / The alien airman dropped and, still half-dazed, / He failed to notice the old bull that grazed / A dozen yards away, until the brute, Startled to anger by such insolence, / With frothing muzzle lifted suddenly / Let out a bellow and, crashing through the fence / Charged head-down at his country's enemy.
—Wilfrid Gibson

In his 1953 book *Sailor Malan*, historian and author Oliver Walker wrote:

". . . the public of Britain and the Commonwealth, starved of any territorial successes and bowed down-by the enormity of Germany's conquests, was not to be denied its heroes. Fighter pilots embodied their spirit of defiance and their belief in ultimate victory. There was comfort too, for Britain, in the presence among these pilots of men who had come thousands of miles to fight for the Old Country. It made them

feel less alone, more aware of resources of blood and kin far
beyond the reach of the rain of bombs."

LEGEND

Air Chief Marshal H.C.T. Dowding: "I probably knew Sailor better than I knew most officers serving in squadrons during that time of stress which has become known as the Battle of Britain. I looked on him as one of the great assets of the Command—a fighter pilot who was not solely or mainly concerned with his own 'score', but as one whose first thoughts were for the efficiency of his squadron, and the personal safety of his junior pilots who fought under his command. I know that he was regarded as a heroic figure by the small fry over whom he spread his influence, and I personally shared their opinion."

Bullet grazes and other wounds and combat-related injuries of all degrees were common to most of the fighter pilots in that summer and autumn. A number of 74's pilots were attended by personnel at Southend-on-Sea General Hospital and the house surgeon there at the time, Geoffrey Flavell, remembered: "We saw a great deal of them in our hospital Mess. I recall H. M. Stephen saying to me: 'You know, Doc, my trouble is I can't shoot straight, even when I get the beggars in line. Now Sailor there never misses them!'

"Sailor would never talk freely as did the others. I found him (leaning silently against the mantelpiece, a pint of beer in his hand which did him the whole evening) rather difficult to know, and exceedingly uncommunicative. As he had already established a reputation as a killer, and his silent stolidity was so much at variance with the extroversion of the others I was at some pains to draw him out, and on one occasion devoted a whole evening to doing so.

'Tell me, Sailor, as a matter of technical interest, how exactly do you go about shooting down a bomber?'

After some rumination: 'I try not to now.'

'Whatever do you mean?'

'Well, I think it's a bad thing.'

'Now come, Sailor, I really want to know. Don't trifle with me.'

'I mean it. I think it's a thoroughly bad thing. You see, if you shoot them down they don't get back and no one in Germany is a wit the wiser. So I figure the right thing to do is to let them get back. With a dead rear gunner; a dead navigator, and the pilot coughing his lungs up as he lands. I think if you do that it has a better effect on their morale. That's what we want to aim at now. Of course, if you just mean to shoot them down, well, what I generally do is . . . knock out port and starboard engines. But, honestly, Doc, the other way is best.' "

Captain Cuthbert Orde distinguished himself as one of the great war artists of all time with the powerful and moving drawings he made of many pilots in Royal Air Force Fighter Command during the Second World War.

Of then-Squadron Leader Adolph G. Malan, D.S.O. and Bar, D.S.C. and Bar, whose portrait Captain Orde made on December 29th 1940, the artist wrote: "All would agree that 'Sailor' Malan is the outstanding Fighter pilot of the war. He is our top scorer with twenty-nine confirmed victories. I have seldom been more impressed by anyone than by him the first time I saw him. A very strong face, a very quiet manner, and an air of authority made it obvious that here was a leader of great determination and ability, with a very sincere personality. 'Sailor' was in the South African Merchant Service for eight years, and joined the RAF about nine years ago. He is married and has a son, to whom the Prime Minister recently stood godfather. I mention that because when I was painting him he told me that having a wife and son had been of the greatest moral help to him during the Battle of Britain, that it gave him an absolutely definite thing to fight for and defend, and that this was his constant thought. His skill, courage, and fighting qualities may be taken for granted: they're obviously facts and are shared by many others, but his character is shared by few. I do not think that Malan could join a squadron without improving it, however good it was. Not by sword-waving, but by a strength of mind and integrity that are at once recognizable and effective. Don't imagine from this that he never laughs; but he has a serious mind and is intent on winning the war."

In mid-June 1940, Sailor's wife Lynda had given birth to their first child, a boy called Jonathan, in a nursing home at Westcliff-on-Sea, near Southend. On a warm summer evening after they had brought the baby home, searchlights scanned the sky and the occasional anti-aircraft guns boomed. Sailor was unable to sleep and finally, he asked permission to take off by himself.

Sailor's rigger and fitter were awakened from a sound sleep and, still in pyjamas, grabbed their rifles and their tin hats, and reported for duty at the dispersal post on the airfield.

They started the Spitfire as Sailor buckled his parachute harness. He climbed into the cockpit and was assisted in strapping himself in before opening up the throttle a little to warm the engine. Glancing upward he spotted an He 111 that had been coned by the field searchlights. It was heading directly across towards him at about 6,000 feet.

Leaving the Spitfire to warm itself up, he leapt from the cockpit with his parachute on and dove into a nearby trench. He remembered the trench as being only a foot and a half deep, but on landing in the thick mud at the bottom, he found that the trench had since been dug to a five foot depth. As he hit bottom, the Heinkel bomber arrived overhead. When the German passed over, Sailor raced back to the waiting Spitfire and roared into the night sky after the intruder. He took off and made straight for the same Heinkel, which was obviously blinded by the searchlights. He caught up with the bomber as it was climbing slowly across the coast.

He quickly closed on the Heinkel and signalled to the anti-aircraft guns (by flashing a succession of dots on his downward recognition light) to cease their firing while he got in position to attack the German. The guns fell silent and he bore in to just fifty yards from the prey. Too close. Firing a three-second burst he had to jam his stick forward to avoid collision with the bomber. His windscreen was soon covered with oil from the Heinkel, which now entered a slow spiral and fell out of the searchlight beams. It crashed on the beach, half in and half out of the water.

Banking to head back to base, he noticed another He 111 in the glare of the searchlights. Again he signalled the guns to hold off as he climbed to align the Spitfire on the enemy. The two aircraft were at 16,000 feet and this time he would not risk overrunning the enemy plane. At 200 yards and closing to 100 yards, he began firing. The Heinkel burst into flames, and a parachute became entangled near the tail. The burning bomber slipped off into a steep spiral and crashed in a vicar's garden near Chelmsford in an enormous sheet of flame.

Back on the ground at Hornchurch, Sailor telephoned his wife. She and the baby had slept through the entire raid.

"He was a born leader and natural pilot of the first order. Complete absence of balderdash. As far as he was concerned, you either did your job properly, or you were on your way. He inspired his air crews by his dynamic and forceful personality, and by the fact that he set such a high standard in his flying."

— Pilot Officer William M. Skinner, No 74 Squadron

"The South African 'Sailor' Malan ended the war as one of
the top-scoring aces on the Allied side. He was important
too, for the influence he had upon RAF tactics and formations. He was a man of burly build with an amiable smile that
made men who met him unready for the deep and clinical
hatred that he had for his German opponents. He told one of
his fellow officers that to badly damage enemy bombers—so
that they arrived home with dead and dying aboard—was
better than shooting them down; it had more effect on
Luftwaffe morale. So that is what he tried to do."
— Len Deighton in *Fighter*

Flying Officer Roger Boulding recalled that, during the win-
ter of '40 and the spring of '41, Sailor was instrumental in
introducing and leading the 'trailing our coats' operations
over France in an effort to lure the enemy fighters up so the
pilots of 74 would have a chance to knock 'em down.
Boulding flew as Sailor's Number Two on several of these
sweeps from Manston across the Channel to France and found
him always full of determination. His pilots knew him to be
tough and generally a hard man to fly with. "His demeanor
was quiet and very cool. He seemed to have himself very
much under control and never got very excited on the
ground. Whilst he would often have a few quiet beers in the
evening with the rest of us, he was never a great party goer.
Everyone held him in very great esteem and had great confidence in his leadership, even if they were not always keen on
his methods of stirring up trouble."

As it was his own squadron, Sailor normally led the Biggin
wing with 74 Squadron. He was leading on the trip in which
Boulding was shot down. It was a clear day and the squadron
had crossed the French coast. Boulding was leading one section of four and spotted a formation of Me109s, with the
famous yellow-painted noses, climbing towards the Spitfires.

Boulding radioed the sighting to Sailor who led the pilots in a diving turn straight onto the Germans. Boulding followed one down in a near vertical dive but had to break off without seemingly causing major damage to the enemy aircraft. Sailor radioed the pilots to reform. Boulding flew slightly behind him, both of them using the tactic of flying towards the sun in a weaving pattern to present a difficult target.

Boulding looked behind and spotted another Spitfire following him in the same fashion. Then Sailor began to call for someone to 'look-out behind!' and urgently to take evasive action. Boulding looked back and saw what he thought was the same aircraft guarding his rear and began to hunt round for the one in trouble. He had just spotted a Spitfire rocking its wings violently (probably Sailor) when his aircraft was hit from behind. The armour plate behind his seat took the blow and saved him. The aileron controls were damaged and the stick just flopped from side to side without effect. His Spitfire went into a spiral dive from about 25,000 feet, and he had to get out fast. He pulled the canopy release and undid his seat straps but could not get out because of the spinning. He had to get his knee up and jerk the stick forward, which effectively catapulted him out. He pulled the ripcord and parachuted down from somewhere above 10,000 feet. The Germans had ample time to reach him when he landed and before he could stand up there were plenty of them threatening him with an assortment of weapons.

Flight Lieutenant R.M.B. Duke-Woolley: "I knew Sailor off and on for some years. He was a very nice man, not at all the swashbuckler which one or two other aces could well be called. He was at Biggin Hill, of course, in 1940 while I was at Kenley. He was about average at Staff College, tending to be too modest to thump the table—as others might have done with his reputation. I think he was a hunter, really. Good shot, indifferent to danger and with the same killing instinct as a professional hunter."

The highest-scoring RAF fighter ace of the war, Johnnie Johnson, on Sailor: "I never served with him, and my contacts were limited to attending his various lectures and meeting him socially on various occasions when he was commanding Biggin Hill. Nevertheless, in the dark days of 1940 he soon became a legendary figure in Fighter Command and was a great inspiration to all young fighter pilots who first joined fighter squadrons at that time.

"Sailor Malan shot down thirty-two enemy aeroplanes before I opened my account, and our fighting days bear little comparison, for Sailor, like Manfred von Richthofen, fought defensively when the odds were heavy against him, while I, like Mick Mannock, nearly always fought over Europe with a squadron or wing behind me."

David Masters points out in *So Few* the understated nature and sparing use of adjectives in official citations for military awards, and notes specific exceptions in the glowing references of Sailor Malan's Distinguished Service Order and Bar, and Distinguished Flying Cross and Bar citations relative to his "magnificent leadership" and his "brilliant leadership", as well as his "exceptional skill and courage as a pilot". By inference, much of Sailor's success in combat is attributable to his perspective about 'the Squadron'. The Squadron is what counts, the team, not the individual, and the importance of infusing a team spirit into the Squadron, that was what turned No 74 Squadron into the "band of cool, resourceful, fearless fighter pilots whose toll of the German Luftwaffe by the end of 1940 raised them to eminence in the Royal Air Force."

A uniquely efficient leader, Sailor knew instinctively how to inspire and get the best, and the most, out of his men. He made certain they knew why they were there—to shoot down Germans without being shot down themselves. On the way to building his standard of efficiency into the Squadron, Sailor made sure they understood the two things he would not tolerate were incompetence and lack of decision. The lesson of air combat was and is, one must be decisive. Get in, attack, get out. Better a poor decision than no decision.

Historian / author Stephen Bungay on Sailor: "There was, by all accounts, something deeply impressive about this man. He was modest and unfussy, an expert and a professional, but above all a team-builder. He was not interested in scores, although when the battle ended he was the RAF's top-scorer. One of his flight commanders, Harbourne Mackay Stephen, has commented: 'I don't really know how many I shot down. Much has been written about the competition between individuals in their quest to be top scorer. Such competition in my experience did not exist. We all did our job, which was to destroy as many of the enemy as we could. If the opportunity presented itself then we took it as an individual, a section or a squadron . . .We were not in there for personal glory but as part of a team, and in 74's case a very well disciplined team.' "

London *Daily Express*: "The brilliant battle career of Adolph Gysbert Malan . . . is now at an end. He has fought his last fight. The fighter ace is going home to pass on his skill to young airmen. In a polo pullover and a Mae West he led the battered RAF squadrons that saved the world, from an airfield on the fringe of London. They were seldom opposed by fewer than ten to one. But they held, and Malan is one of the few who has lived to fight the battle in reverse. His accomplishments will never be dimmed."

He made a final visit to the White Hart at Brasted, near Biggin Hill, before leaving England in 1946. It was a farewell visit to old friends, during which he unveiled a special memorial in the bar, the now oak-framed blackout screen on which so many prominent RAF fighter pilots and commanders had scrawled their signatures in chalk. The signatures were now treated with a preservative and the framed board protected with heavy glass. It bore the names of Sailor, Al Deere, Jamie Rankin, Bob Stanford Tuck, Michael Crossley, Geoffrey Page, Brian Kingcome, Colin Gray, Johnny Kent, Tony Bartley and others. Sailor spoke to those who had gathered: "My feelings are very mixed. This is a happy occasion in some ways, and I am trying to smile. But it would be a strange man who didn't have sadder thoughts when he reads some of these names and remembers. We built up a 'Fighter' tradition that will not easily die. I hope you will all come here often to steep yourselves in a bit of tradition."

On September 27th 1963, Adolph G. Malan died of pneumonia and Parkinson's Disease at Kimberley, South Africa, aged 52. In 1966, members of 74 Squadron conceived a memorial for Sailor, the Malan Memorial Sword. It was made by Wilkinson and, on the evening of July 15th 1966, the magnificent trophy was presented to the squadron at Bentley Priory, the great house on the hill above Stanmore, north of London, that had been the headquarters of RAF Fighter Command in the Second World War. Accompanying the sword were the wonderful portrait of Sailor, by Cuthbert Orde, and a drawing of two Spitfires in the markings of 74 Squadron, by Group Captain Norman Hoad. The speech was made by Group Captain D.S. Brookes: "The presentation of the Sword is made by twenty-eight former members of the

Squadron in the years 1936-45 and I am deeply honoured to represent them tonight.

"Sailor was, I think, the outstanding fighter pilot of World War Two and accounted for over thirty enemy aircraft confirmed destroyed and another twenty probably destroyed. He joined 74 on the day he left his Flying Training School, as an Acting Pilot Officer, and served in all ranks until on 8th August 1940, at the height of the Battle of Britain, he assumed command as a Squadron Leader. He left only when promoted to Wing Commander on 9th March 1941, to become Wing Leader of the Fighter Wing in which the Squadron flew, but he continued to fly with 74. In fact, was never in any other Squadron, so it seems entirely appropriate that this presentation should be a family affair of past and present members of Tiger Squadron.

"From a personal point of view, I find the most endearing thing about him was that, apart from being an exceptional shot, he was just an ordinary chap; quiet, unassuming, and gentle in manner. His great gifts came from within when great gifts were called for. Tremendous courage, relentless determination and that quality of leadership which carried the whole Squadron to great deeds with him. For in those dark but glorious days the record of the Squadron in battle was, as in 1918, second to none.

"This small book which, for want of a better name, we call the Charter, is devised to place the presentation on record and to act as a record of subsequent changes of command, when the custody of the Sword will devolve upon the new commander. It also ensures that in years to come no young member of the Squadron need ever ask: 'Who was this chap Malan and what did he do?' "

TORCH COMMANDO

In 1946, Sailor Malan retired from the Royal Air Force and returned to his native South Africa with his wife and children. In the war years they had shared twenty-nine homes, little furnished flats mostly, all located near the airfields on which Sailor had served. Like a good air force wife, Lynda Malan accepted the rootless existence of their wartime movements and adjusted to the risk and danger of her husband's job. "I didn't worry at first. It was only towards the end I began to be really afraid that something might, and could, happen . . . after all."

Before he left England, Sailor was introduced by friends to Sir Ernest Oppenheimer and his son, Harry, who headed a vast empire of gold mining, diamond, chemical and copper companies, the largest being Anglo-American Corporation Ltd, whose headquarters was in Johannesburg. Sailor and Harry got on well, and were nearly the same age. Like Sailor, Harry had had an action-packed wartime career, as a captain in the 4th Armoured Car Regiment, the famous Desert Rats, in North Africa. The two men shared many common values as well as a profound loyalty to their South African home-land. The friendship with Oppenheimer led to an invitation for Sailor to join the staff of the Anglo-American Corporation in Johannesburg. "I don't know what it will be until I have a try-out and see where I fit in. A change of job is always excit-ing. I've tried the sea and the air. Now it's time I tried the land."

Prosperity and opportunity were developing in South Africa immediately after the war and the United Party government of General Smuts was grateful for the wartime contributions of the nation's many military veterans. His government helped them to find jobs, start businesses, buy homes and cars. Many people in the misery of war-torn Europe looked to the sunshine and promise of South Africa for a new start. Politically, though, Dr. Daniel Malan's opposition Nationalist Party with its racist policies, cast a threatening cloud over the country's future. In 1940, when Sailor was fighting the Battle of Britain, Daniel Malan (his distant cousin) spoke to the South African House of Assembly of his belief that Adolf Hitler would win the war and would then grant South Africa her long-sought status as a republic.

Dr Malan's supporters perpetuated the base hatreds of the Boer wars, and not only England, but also Capitalism, Liberalism, Jewry, and a list of other menacing 'threats' fuelled their manifesto. Their bible was the daily *Die Transvaler*, a newspaper which the courts had declared "a tool of the Nazis." They briefly had the support and protection of a group called the Action Front, an organization with a core of storm trooper types, until the AF became so large and powerful in its own right that it began to threaten Dr Malan's authority.

Sailor, meanwhile, was welcomed back to his country, and to Johannesburg, with great enthusiasm for the war hero that he was. He was made private and political secretary to his friend, Harry Oppenheimer, and was soon integrated into the heady atmosphere of the city's golf and private clubs. He immersed himself into learning about Anglo-American's business. "It's fascinating work. There's an awful lot to learn and a chap's got to be on his toes. But it's the greatest opportunity I've ever had. I hope I make good. I hope Russia doesn't get too tough. I don't want to lose all this. I prefer the sky just plain blue."

In the general election of May 1948, Daniel Malan's Nationalists squeaked into power with a narrow win and set out to "Afrikanerize" the country and spread the policies of "Apartheid" and white supremacy far and wide as quickly as possible.

They began with an immediate crackdown on immigration, confiscated the passports of those who had offended the Nationalists, purged government departments of heads with English surnames, released inmates who had been imprisoned for treason, denied citizens access to the courts, and redesigned uniforms to eliminate any similarity to British tradition.

Harry Oppenheimer was a member of the South African Parliament and his position afforded Sailor a close-up view of the new government in action, a display he found most unsavoury. Sailor's strong belief in democracy, which had so powerfully driven him in the fight against the Nazis and Fascism, now drove him into action again. He discussed his views with Oppenheimer and concluded that he needed to make some changes in his life and act on his more deep-seated beliefs.

Sailor and his wife settled on Benfontein, a farm eight miles from Kimberley. There he had 27,000 acres, a shooting reserve with buck, wildebeeste, wild duck, blue cranes, guinea fowl and small game birds, as well as good grazing for the 900 sheep he purchased. He had plans to add a dairy herd in the paddocked area too. The house needed a lot of work, paint and repairs, and considerable attention to the garden and orchards, all chores relished by Lynda and Sailor. They liked Kimberley. It was cosy and unpretentious, if a bit shabby, and it had good schools for their children. Life there offered what Sailor was looking for—until March 1951, when Dr Daniel Malan's government announced the Separate Representation of Coloured Voters Act, a measure which would disenfranchise the Cape coloured voters in violation of the Act of Union. This blatant flaunting of the Constitution infuriated thousands of South Africans, including many ex-servicemen. Meetings were soon organized and an "Action

Committee for the Defence of the Constitution" was formed. Secessionist talk was rampant. A Rand War Veterans Action Committee was organized and they planned a torchlight procession and march through the streets of Johannesburg to City Hall for a "Hands off the Constitution" rally.

The spirit of the protest was spreading rapidly around the country and Sailor was caught up in the fervour. It appealed to his principles and when he was invited by the organizers of the Johannesburg rally to come and speak, he accepted enthusiastically. He was greeted there by dozens of banners and shouts of the thousands of people attending: "We Demand a General Election", "No Surrender," "Away with Totalitarianism," and "The Coloured Vote Goes First—Then the English Language." When it was Sailor's turn to speak, he said: "The strength of this gathering is evidence that the men and women who fought in the war for freedom still cherish what they fought for. We are determined not to be denied the fruits of that victory. It is good to see this support in protest against the rape of the Constitution and the attack on our rights and liberties as free men. In Abyssinia, at Alamein and a score of bloody campaigns, we won the right to a voice in our country's affairs. And we are determined that our voice shall not only be heard but that it shall also be heeded. This Bill has been foisted on us in the so-called name of the people—the broad will of the people. We do not like this Bill, and we are the people."

At first, the government response to the campaign of the war veterans and the United Party, was to sneer and belittle the effort of the campaigners, but when mass parades of cars and jeeps converged on Parliament in Cape Town, carrying hundreds of celebrated war veterans, retired generals, judges, lawyers and well-known sports figures, the Nationalists counterattacked. Mustering their toadying press, Dr Malan and his associates mounted a campaign of their own, to smear and discredit the veterans and their followers as hooligans. They then went after the anti-government leadership, Sailor Malan and others, branding them stooges of Oppenheimer Ltd and perfidious capitalism; a bizarre allegation in light of the government's other principal claim, that the war veterans were tools of the communists.

Another pro-government paper, *Die Burger*, wrote: "The infallible instinct of anti-Nationalist English-speaking elements to range themselves behind leaders who are regarded as Afrikaans, remains a source of amazement to the Nationalists . . . the organizing committee behind recent demonstrations remains overwhelmingly English-speaking. But the two main figures are Afrikaners, an Afrikaans veteran ('*outstryder*'—old fighter), and a member of an Afrikaans family whose real fame rests on his role in the 'Battle of Britain' . . . the real Kommandant General is without doubt Sailor Malan."

Sailor was, in fact, elected National President at the conference of the war veterans, now called the Torch Commando, held in June 1951. A torch was adopted as the organization's iconic symbol. Torch Commando was established as a pressure group with the goal of ousting the Nationalist government by lawful, constitutional means. By forming small committees to spread the truth about the Nationalists to the ordinary folk in the towns across the country, and using Sailor to speak at these gatherings, it hoped to influence the population. They established a constitution of their own with five main principles:
1. To uphold the spirit of the solemn compacts entered upon at the time of Union as moral obligations of trust and honour binding upon Parliament and the people. 2. To secure the repeal of any measures enacted in violation of such obligations. 3. To protect the freedom of the individual in worship, language, and speech and to ensure his right of free access

to the Courts. 4. To eliminate all forms of totalitarianism whether Fascist or Communist. 5. To promote racial harmony in the Union.

Early in the campaign, Sailor provoked wide-reaching reaction when he asked that pro-Nationalist press reporters be excluded from the anti-government meetings. He knew they would seize upon and distort Torch Commando plans to field mobile units: "We are militant, not military", in support of their efforts. Dr Daniel Malan reacted in a speech: "People contend that the Torch Commando will go a little way and then vanish. That is not my view. The Torch Commando is to be taken seriously because it has a military or semi-military character. Private armies of that nature cannot be tolerated . . . If they make their appearance at Nationalist Party meetings, as they have begun to do, you can well understand that there will be a reaction on the part of the Nationalists . . ." Many confrontations followed.

For Sailor, the experience of carrying the message of the Torch all round the country was a strangely ambivalent one. He was gratified and flattered by the admiring responses he received at most of the appearances he made, but discomforted by the often less than subtle pressures both within and without the movement, to further politicize their policies and aims. In the course of his speaking engagements, he encountered considerable criticism for a lack of fluency in the Afrikaans language, much of which he had lost through lack of use in the war years. He had to brush up on it as it was essential for campaigning in the rural areas. Objectively, he was less comfortable sitting at conference tables helping to plan strategy, programmes and policy, and less comfortable with the pace of the movement, as the Nationalists were forging ahead with their own plans to "Afrikanerize" South Africa.

Meanwhile the Parliament was in session, with a pending

Supreme Court decision on whether the Nationalist government of Dr Malan had violated the terms of the Act of Union when it forced through the Separate Representation of Voters Act on a simple majority. Four black voters had brought legal action against the Act—an action that had failed. It had then been brought to the high court on appeal. While awaiting the appeal decision, Sailor and the other leaders of Torch met to agree on the formation of a United Democratic Front: "Torch is not worried about the Appeal Court judgement. That is the legal aspect. We're concerned about the moral side. To us the Act is unconstitutional. Therefore, whatever happens, our determination to kick the Nationalist government out is unchanged."

The Supreme Court ruled the Act invalid as it violated the Act of Union. The court said that coloured voters could not be placed on a separate register by this means, and were entitled to remain on the common roll. Daniel Malan: "It is clear that the situation which has now arisen is an intolerable one and the Government would be grossly neglecting its duty towards the people and towards a democratically-elected Parliament if steps are not taken to put an end to this confusing and dangerous situation. It is imperative that the legislative sovereignty of Parliament should be placed beyond any doubt in order to ensure order and certainty. The Governement will take the necessary steps to do its duty, and will, at the appropriate time, announce such steps after the reasons for the judgement have been studied and considered."

The loss of confidence in the government brought no resignation or announcement of new elections by Dr Malan, but it stirred in the people talk of secession, civil disobedience, even civil war. His ministers began hinting that the government would ban the Torch Commando. Dr Malan himself decried the Oppenheimers as the "money-power" behind

Torch Commando and the United Party opposition to the government and apartheid. The government had scores of police detectives brought in to Cape Town to protect the cabinet ministers. The Cape branch of Torch stated: "The drafting of police reinforcements to Cape Town is an amateurish effort at employing psychological warfare against the Torch Commando. The Torch Commando has nothing to fear and refuses to be intimidated for its belief that this government is heading towards a virtual dictatorship." Finally, as the parliamentary session was nearing an end, Dr Malan's administration devised and forced through an Act called the High Court of Parliament Bill, which canceled the Supreme Court appeal ruling and declared that parliamentarians were the only persons competent to sit in judgement of their own acts.

The next local election resulted in increased support for the Nationalists, support coming from the farmer's of the flatlands. Some influential anti-Nationalist speakers began calling for the United Party to stop trying to be all things to all voters, to forget the flatlanders and focus on being an urban party that catered to the interests of capital and labour as the country was becoming more and more industrialized. But the leadership of Torch Commando took a rather different view, passing a new resolution at its July congress convened in Pretoria: "That for the Torch Commando to abandon the rural areas would be a tactical error of the first magnitude. It agrees that a committee of rural representatives meet should immediately, or as soon as possible after this congress, to outline the policy that should be pursued in Operation Backveld."

Sailor had been a farmer in his own country for less than a year, much of that time spent on the road working for the principles of the anti-Nationalist movement. Torch Commando membership was now more than 234,000 and its immediate priorities were canvassing for funds and house-to-house visits to make converts to the cause ahead of the April date for the next general election, which had finally been set by Dr Malan.

As the country moved inexorably towards that election, Sailor and the other Torch leaders declared that the movement would fade away after the election. There was some talk of the United Party absorbing Torch entirely before then. Douglas Mitchell, an ambitious former administrator of Natal Province, believed he could parlay with the Nationalists, as the "virtual leader of English-speaking South Africa." He saw Torch Commando as a renegade influence and a real danger in the possibility of it parting company with United Party policy which, he thought, would automatically cost the UP twelve seats in the House, and the general election in April. But the leaders of Torch were showing signs of disillusionment with the United Party about whether the UP leadership had the drive, the magnetism, or even the proper machinery to win the election. The Torch leadership questioned too, whether, assuming the United Party were to win the election, it would be safe to dissolve Torch, leaving the future of the country in the hands of political leaders who had failed before?

Die Burger editorialized: "The movement [Torch] rejects the Nationalist policy. It does not accept the United Party's policy, presumably because, like ourselves, it is unable to find out exactly what that policy is. But from the Torch Commando we expect to hear a clear call to action which will bring a renewal to the country's political life. But what is it to be? The only clear opposing system of thought to the Nationalist 'apartheid' policy is liberalism. But will the Commando nail their flag to its mast and fight the battle on clearly formulated principles, or will it shrink from the choice as the United Party has done?

"If the Commando shrinks from the choice of liberalism, then it has taken the first step towards losing the idealism which fed the flames of the torch. Then the way is open for another compromise and yet another; compromise at each point at which it has to make a choice until in the end it becomes quite indistinguishable from the United Party, which it had come to rejuvenate. If the movement chooses the path of liberalism, however, it runs the risk of losing its followers and lessening its prospects of immediate success. It also runs the risk of estranging itself from the United Party and bringing about such a division in opposition circles which would lessen the chances of political success even more greatly [as began to happen in 1952]. It is no wonder then that the Commando hesitates and takes postponing resolutions. One can have sympathy with it in its first acquaintance with hard political realities. But he who wants to achieve political success must be ready to support brave words with brave deeds. The Torch must have a wick, other-wise it will not burn for long."

It was a fact that virtually all the leaders of Torch were part-time activists, farmers (like Sailor), lawyers, businessmen, who all preferred to leave politics to the politicians. The historian Oliver Walker: "What are Sailor's personal feelings towards this challenge? He is a young man (forty-two) and in robust health. Politics intrigue him a little even if he does not like the way they are managed. There is a safe seat waiting for him any time he likes to abandon the Torch Commando for the United Party. He has no profoundly-reasoned programme of reforms, social and economic, such as his country needs. His creed is very simple: 'I believe in leadership.' "

In Walker's view, South Africa had two distinct kinds of Afrikaner: the sectional Volk, traditional and tribal, exulting in their brief top-doggism, and the evolved South African,

who may be of either English or Afrikaans stock, but who has
respect for both, the sort of ideal new citizen that Generals
Louis Botha and Jan Christiaan Smuts envisaged when they
signed the peace treaty of Vereeniging in 1902 and the Act of
Union in 1910. He believed Sailor to be as good an example
as one could find of the breed, pointing out that there were
thousands like him. "European South Africa has no other
future unless it produces more and more in the same superi-
or mould."

TIME magazine, September 27th, 1963: "Died. Group Captain
Adolph Gysbert Malan, 52, one of World War II's top air
aces, South African merchant sailor who traded his sea legs
for wings, bagged 35 Nazi planes as an RAF Spitfire pilot,
returned home to organize 250,000 war veterans into the
'Torch Commando,' which disbanded in 1953 after an unsuccessful campaign to change the racist policies of Prime
Minister Daniel Malan, a distant relative; of pneumonia, in
Kimberley, South Africa."

AUTHOR'S NOTE
Sailor Malan referred to himself as a simple man. During the
Battle of Britain and his challenging days of combat in the
months and years that followed, his reputation was that of a
ruthless, calculating killer in the air. Oliver Walker's 1953
biography of Sailor notes that: "today the idea amuses
him; he throws it out with a look of inquiry. He would admit
that he was different in those days. Who would not have
been, with death breathing down your neck daily, or the neck
of the man who flew beside you? No pilot on operations could
afford the luxury of grief or regrets. Few of them who stayed
as long on combat duty as Sailor were altogether normal. A
man had to build a cocoon around himself, a resistance."
Sailor: 'My wife says I was a maniac in those days,' he can

say reflectively. I prefer the words of one citation for an award that speaks of his 'disdain' in the face of the enemy. A good pilot could only survive by a mixture of disdain and eternal vigilance."

The Battle of Britain produced many airmen of great skill and accomplishment; high-achievers who made their mark in one of history's most memorable and demanding campaigns. But only a few of them distinguished themselves in such a way as to become legends in their own lifetimes. Among the greatest of these was Sailor Malan.

REMEMBERING SAILOR

Al Deere: "To say I was bitterly disappointed when, on finishing at the Staff College, I found myself returned to 13 Group headquarters as a staff officer, would be a gross under-statement of my feelings. Optimistically, I had hoped to be returned to flying, even perhaps as a wing leader. My spirits were very low, and I thought that, for me, the active war was over. Victor Beamish's words, on my departure from Kenley when I was on the crest of the wave, often came to mind: 'Al, if you never do another operation in this war, you/ve done more than your share.' Repeatedly, I told myself that I should be satisfied, I had done my share—why not sit back, enjoy life, take it easy and let other fools get shot down. But, the gnawing desire to return to flying was ever present.

"In February I saw my chance to take a step forward. 'Daddy' Bouchier, now an Air Commodore, arrived at 13 Group headquarters as S.A.S.O., and I appealed to him, to allow me a two weeks' attachment at Biggin Hill, where 'Sailor' Malan was now installed as Station Commander. 'After all,' I pleaded, 'an air staff officer must keep up to date with current operations.' I knew I could fix it with 'Sailor'—in fact, I had already got his verbal agreement—and it was merely a question of being allowed away from the Group for two weeks. I think memories of 54 Squadron and Hornchurch won the day, for 'Daddy' gave his consent.

"At Biggin Hill, Dicky Milne, who was the wing leader, arranged for me to fly as a member of 611 Squadron. I knew how squadron commanders hated supernumeraries in their squadron and I was careful therefore not to stake my claims to leadership but to fly when, and in whatever position in the formation, the

squadron commander or his flight commanders wished.
As a result, I found myself flying as a number two, as a
number three and in any stooge position in the squadron
where there was a gap to be filled. To be frank, I can't
say I was happy going through the mill again, as it were,
especially having been a leader since the early days of
the war. Nevertheless, I was exhilarated, in a curious
sort of way, for the first time since the fateful day over
Le Touquet with 403 Squadron.

"At all costs I had to bag myself a Hun; somehow I
felt that a flying appointment depended on it. When my
fourteen days were up I hadn't fired a shot in anger.
The weather had been bad throughout the period, and
the wing had been on only a few abortive shows. On two
occasions I managed to get myself on a 'Rhubarb' (that
useless and hated operation) but even then without success; although on one occasion, when flying as a number three in a section of four, we did manage to surprise
some F.W. 190s but we were not quite quick enough to
catch them and, using their superior speed at low level,
they avoided combat.

"With 'Sailor's' connivance I decided to stay on for
a few more days and risk the wrath of 'Daddy' on my
return to 13 Group. Two days later I was in combat. I
was leading a section in the wing when at 37,000 feet
over St. Omer I sighted a dozen F.W. 190s some ten
thousand feet below. I called Dicky Milne and told him
I was taking my section down to attack. As we neared
the enemy fighters they saw us and split. I singled out
one, determined at all costs to get him. I had speed and
height in my favour and, in contrast to the ill-fated battle with 403 Squadron, I was behind the controls of a
Spitfire IX which was superior to the F.W. 190 above
25,000 feet. To me, the fight that ensued was more

important than any that had gone before—my future was at stake. I felt like a boxer entering the ring before a big fight, tense and breathless, and curiously excited. As my cannons found their mark, and bits from the disintegrating Focke-Wulf hurtled past my aircraft, there was no exhilaration at victory, no sorrow at killing, no revenge for past hurts, but merely a sense of achievement—this is what I had set out to do, and I had done it. 'Sailor' was delighted at my success. After two more uneventful days at Biggin, I was ordered to return to 13 Group.

" 'I'm sorry, Al, but you'll have to return,' said 'Sailor' as I faced him in his office where I had gone to plead for one more day's flying. 'The Group Captain Operations at 13 Group has been on the phone and he says there can be no further extension.'

" 'Oh well, if that's the case I'd better be on my way. Thanks for having me,' I answered ruefully.

" 'Don't give up, Al, I'll keep plugging your case. You can come here any time you like and fly with the wing.'

"Installed again in my office at 13 Group, I felt that I had played my last card, and lost. Three days later I was summoned to 'Daddy's' office to be greeted by a S.A.S.O., all smiles.

" 'You've made it, Al, and let me say how pleased I am. You have been posted to command the Kenley Wing with effect Monday next. Congratulations and the very best of luck.'

"I reported for my interview with Air Vice-Marshal Saunders on the Monday, as instructed, only to find that the posting had been changed and I was to become the wing leader at Biggin Hill. In between my appointment to Kenley and arrival at Group headquarters

Dicky Milne had been shot down. Apparently 'Sailor' had forthwith phoned the A.O.C. and asked for me to replace Dicky, not knowing that I had already been appointed to Kenley. The A.O.C. kindly agreed to switch. Thus it came about that I was appointed to command the famous Biggin Hill Wing, and Johnny Johnson was promoted to fill the vacancy at Kenley. I felt I was now on the crest of the wave again.

"During the time I was out of circulation I had thought a great deal about wing tactics and now that I had at last realized my ambition to become a wing leader there were a number of changes I proposed to introduce at Biggin. In 'Sailor' Malan as Station Commander I had, to my way of thinking, the best fighter tactician and leader produced by the R.A.F. in World War II. I was anxious therefore to put my theories to him in order to get his approval and support before putting them into practice. On the very first day of my new command I presented myself in 'Sailor's' office and launched forthwith into the subject of wing tactics.

" 'You're the wing leader,' he said, 'and the tactics you adopt are entirely a matter for you to decide. Naturally, I'm interested but I have no intention of interfering unless things go wrong. But go ahead, I'd like to hear what you've got to say.'

"I had destroyed the 995th aircraft for Biggin Hill. Three days later the total still stood at 995. Bad weather had again interfered with operations, and continued to do so until the 14th May. On this day we were heavily engaged over Courtrai and Jack Charles and his number two each destroyed a F.W. 190, while Chris Martell sent a Me 109G to flaming destruction. Two to go. The pilots were gripped by a feverish intensity; none would take leave and all wanted to fly. Apart from the glory of being the lucky pilot to get the 1,000th Hun, there was the added attraction of a £300 cash prize, raised through a mammoth raffle which had been under way for the past six months.

"The 15th May was set fine, and I had a feeling that this was the day. So much so that I telephoned Alan Mitchell, the New Zealand War Correspondent in London and a friend of mine, to ask him out for the day to witness the event. To 'Sailor' I said, 'I think you should come with us today, sir, I feel confident we're going to get among them.'

" 'Since you put it that way, I'll come,' answered 'Sailor'. In the event, the first show took place in the late afternoon and at first sight it looked as if there would be no reaction from the Hun. Twelve Bostons were to bomb Caen airfield and the Biggin Wing was to act as withdrawal cover. At 21,000 feet we swept in over Fecamp, swung around behind Le Havre, crossed the Seine estuary and approached Caen from the east. On the final approach to the target area I could just pick out the retreating bombers, their positions marked by the black balls of bursting flak in their wake, and above and behind them the glinting canopies of their escort. There were no enemy fighters to be seen. As we neared our turning point, and the bombers retreated further out to sea, I wondered if my optimism had been misplaced. But no, just below and to my left two F.W. 190s appeared climbing hard from out of the haze. As Jack Charles was leading the section on that side I ordered him down to attack. He was quick to take advantage of the opportunity, and I saw him sliding in behind the Huns as they disappeared from my view underneath the formation.

" 'Tallyho, going down, Grass-seed Red,' René's voice came over the R/T.

" 'You've got him, Jack.'

" 'Good show, Grass-seed Leader,' Boudier's voice followed so closely on the excited victory chant of Jack's number two that the kills must have been almost simultaneous.

" 'Tuban Yellow Leader to Brutus, both enemy aircraft destroyed,' in a matter of fact voice Jack announced his kills.

" 'I too have one, Brutus,' René, not to be outdone, announced his victory.

"There were no further engagements and the wing returned to Biggin to be met by an excited gathering of officers and airmen.

" 'Who got the thousandth?' asked 'Spy' as I stepped from my aircraft.

" 'Damned if I know, 'Spy', there were three shot down, but it all happened so quickly that I couldn't tell. From the R/T chatter I should say it was a draw. Perhaps 'Sailor' will be able to make a decision. Let's go and see what he says.'

" 'You're a fine one, Al,' said 'Sailor' pointing an accusing finger at me as we approached his aircraft. 'Why the hell didn't you let me go after those Huns? They passed right under my nose.'

" 'And mine too, sir, but Jack was in the best position. I must say I was tempted to have a go myself—I could do with that £300.'

" 'Well, we'll never know for sure who got the one that mattered. I've decided that Jack and René are to share the honour and the money. I think that's the fairest thing to do, don't you, 'Spy'?'

" 'Yes, I'm sure it is, sir,' answered 'Spy' who, more than any other, had looked forward to this great day. So saying, he dashed off to send the many signals and telegrams which he had long since prepared for the occasion.

"Thus it came about that the 1,000th enemy aircraft destroyed by pilots operating from Biggin Hill was shared by a Canadian and a Frenchman, while a South African station commander and a New Zealander wing leader looked on.

"Anyone who said he felt no fear in action was not telling the truth. Youth and inexperience could possibly dull the senses but one quickly discovered that in war it was not all one-sided. The Germans were doing their level best to try and kill or maim you."

Charles Lindbergh, the pioneering American aviator and the first airman to make the 3,000-mile Atlantic alone flight crossing alone, had taken off in his specially-built Ryan *Spirit of St. Louis* on an epic achievement, May 20, 1927, from Curtiss Airfield, New York. Oliver Walker: "Sailor had neither seen a 'plane nor given them a second thought. No personal significance attached to that lone flight. But its impact could not be dodged on his second voyage which brought him to New York at a time when four million Americans choked the city and ticker-taped Wall Street to give the returning airman the greatest reception ever accorded any event since the Armistice of 1918.

"Lindbergh was Sailor's first flesh-and-blood hero. He symbolized two things. Adventure in an unsuspected and uncharted medium. And he was an exemplar of that exhuberant, enterprising, American spirit which exhilarated him as no previous experience ever had. New York was not merely his first foreign port. It was the first foreign land where he had stepped ashore in uniform, and laden with a skipper's bags. He was no longer a mere cadet among cadets. He was a useful member of a firmly-disciplined ship's company manning a veteran of one of the largest fleets flying the British flag.

"New York, like any seaport, had its seamier dockside life—the kind of moral marshland which every seaman stepping ashore in a strange land has to wade through and often gets bogged down in. Three things preserved Sailor from such a quadmire. There was his own youthful selectiveness, and his chronic hardupness (his current resources were about thirty shillings or six dollars a month). And there was the British Apprentice Club which was specially run for apprentices off British ships calling in at New York.

"Mrs Hollon C. Spaulding, who joined the club as resident secretary in 1922, three months after the latch string was first hung out, and who was still working at the same post in 1952, recalled that 'Adolph was rather shy, though he was always popular and had many friends . . . Later, as an officer, he was less shy and full of life and enthusiasm.' Walker: "From time to time Mrs Spaulding had to impress on the boys that the club was not a marriage bureau."

R.A.F. Captain Cuthbert Orde, one of the greatest war artists of the Second World War, made a fine drawing of Sailor Malan, as he did of a number of the legendary Battle of Britain pilots. Of Orde, Air Vice-Marshal J.C. Slessor wrote: "It would indeed have been difficult to find anyone more ideally qualified by temperament, experience and sympathy than 'Turps'—or 'the Captain,' as he is known to hundreds of fighter boys—to draw pictures of the pilots of Fighter Command that will live as a permanent record of the sort of chaps they were and what they looked like. And I think in these drawings he has caught something of their characters, something of the essential selves of the men who have made the British Fighter squadrons incomparably the best in the world.' And, on December 29th, 1940, Cuthbert Orde wrote: "All would agree that 'Sailor' Malan is the outstanding fighter pilot of the war. He is our top scorer with twenty-nine confirmed victories. I have seldom been more impressed by anyone than by him the first time I saw him. A very strong face, a very quiet manner, and an air of authority made it obvious that here was a leader of great determination and ability, with a very sincere personality. 'Sailor' was in the South African Merchant Service for eight years, and joined the R.A.F. about nine years ago. He is married and has a son, to whom the Prime Minister recently stood godfather. I mention that because when I was painting him he told me that having a wife and son had been of the greatest moral help to him during the Battle of Britain, that it gave him an absolutely definite thing to fight for and defend, and that this was his constant thought. His skill, courage and fighting qualities may be taken for granted: they're obviously facts and are shared by many others, but his character is shared by few. I do not think that Malan could join a squadron without improving it, however good it was. Not by sword-waving, but by a strength of mind and integrity that are at once recognizable and effective. Don't imagine from this that he never laughs; but he has a serious mind and is intent on winning the war."

Interviewed by the renowned war correspondent Quentin Reynolds, for *Colliers Weekly* magazine, Sailor discussed the scene over Dunkirk on the day the evacuation began and the Spitfires were stretched to their maximum range:

"The only way we could fly to Dunkirk and have enough juice to spend a few minutes over the battle area was by coasting and flying at sea-level up from Boulogne." When they arrived in the area, more than thirty German bombers with heavy fighter cover were circling at 20,000 feet as they bombed the Dunkirk docks.

Historian and author David Masters: "Official citations are factual, prone to understatement and very sparing in the use of adjectives, so if they go so far as to mention 'his magnificent leadership' and 'his brilliant leadership,' nothing can be more certain than the fact that the officer concerned is an outstanding leader; and if they disclose that he has shot down at least eighteen enemy aircraft, he is assuredly a pilot of exceptional skill and courage—which explains why Wing Commander A.G. Malan has won the D.S.O. and Bar, the D.F.C. and Bar. This fine South African fighter pilot, who trained for the South African navy and joined the Royal Air Force in 1936, was the first airman to shoot down two German bombers in one night over England.

"He is a leader to whom the squadron comes before everything. It is the squadron which counts, and the successes of the squadron that matter. The team spirit which he infused into the pilots whom he led in the days of May 1940, served in time to turn Squadron No. 74 into a band of cool and resourceful and fearless pilots whose toll of the German Luftwaffe by the end of 1940 raised them to eminence in the Royal Air Force. He knew how to handle young men with the temperament of fighter pilots, how to inspire them, how to lead them and draw the best out of them. He instilled into them something of the spirit of the Canadian North-West Mounted Police. When they followed him into battle, each went with the intention of getting his man, It was their duty to shoot down Germans without being shot down themselves, and if the enemy escaped one day they could bide their time and knock him down the next.

"Not until the latter half of May did the South African see a German in the air. Having patrolled the French coast for some days without sighting the enemy, he was sent out from his base to intercept a formation of German bombers whose movements had been notified. The interception was controlled from the base by orders which reached him through the radio-telephone and he altered his course and height according to the information received. Visual evidence in the way of heavy anti-aircraft fire was of considerable help in enabling him to locate the raiders over the French coast.

"He was flying across the top of a great cloud hummock which heaped up in the sky like a snowy peak when he nearly flew into a Heinkel 111. The first German he had ever seen was no more than fifty yards away, while fifty yards further on was a Junkers 88. So fast was he moving that only by prompt handling of the stick could he swerve to avoid the Heinkel.

"Terrified that the German might drop down into the cloud a hundred feet below and escape, the South African did a steep turn on to the tail of the enemy and actually started firing on his side with full bank on. His attack was shattering. 'As I straightened up I saw my bullets pouring in and large pieces flew off him. He belched heavy smoke, his undercart fell out and he fell down into the cloud,' he said afterwars.

"Anxious to deal with the German bombers further ahead, he called his section together, and then sank down into the clouds to stalk the enemy for fifteen miles on a compass course. Flying blindly under the surface of the cloud, just as a submarine moves under the surface of the sea, Wing Commander Malan concluded after a few minutes that it was time to bob up above the cloud surface to have a look round.

"It gave him a second thrill within five minutes, for he came up slap underneath a Junkers 88. A quick glance revealed about ten German bombers ahead. Ordering the other two Spitfires to attack, he let loose on the Junkers 88, which he completely surprised. Opening fire from a distance of a hundred yards, he squeezed the button for six seconds and was amazed to see the Junkers literally blow up in the air. While he was firing, the camera which was synchronized with his guns took photographs of what was happening as his bullets went home, and this film, now historic, was shown on all the newsreels in cinemas all over Great Britain.

"Needless to add, the other two pilots of his section seized their opportunity. One shot down a Junkers before the rest escaped in the clouds, and it transpired that the other, Flight Lieutenant J.C. Freeborn, who now holds the D.F.C. and Bar, managed to shoot down two of the Junkers. Unfortunately he caught a bullet in the radiator which drove him down in France.

"The Germans were over-running the country all round him, but Flight Lieutenant Freeborn was determined to elude them. The first thing he did was to push his Spitfire among the undergrowth where he landed, then he covered it up with branches so tht it was completely concealed not only from the air, but from any passer-by on the ground. Having hidden his Spitfire from prying eyes, he set off to see whether he could secure some petrol to refill his tanks so that he could make the attempt to cross the Channel.

"For three exciting days he dodged the Germans and tried to obtain petrol from the friendly French. Not a drop

of petrol could he obtain. Once he found a German supply
tank full of petrol that was left unattended by the enemy.
Boldly seizing the chance, he slipped into the seat and
drove it off full speed towards the spot where he had hidden his Spitfire. He was just congratulating himself on his
stratagem and concluding that at last he would be able to
get away when he came face to face with a long German
column. Promptly turning the petrol tanker into the ditch,
he bolted for his life.

"His flying start enabled him to get away, and later he
was picked up at Calais by a Blenheim bomber which was
sent out for him with an escort of Spitfires from his own
squadron.

"Another time the squadron came on fifteen
Messerschmitt 109s flying in broken cloud at 8,000 feet.
There was abundant cover for all, and in the mix-up that
followed Flight Lieutenant Freeborn shot down an Me 109
and darted away into a cloud to climb quickly through it.
Directly he poked his nose out of the top he saw three
Messerschmitts diving on him.

"He did not wait. Spinning round, he took a header into
the cloud again and went down and down in a screeching
dive, shaking off his pursuers in the cloud which blanket-
ed him like a dense fog. As he dropped out of the bottom
of the cloud the first thing he saw was a Messerschmitt
109 chasing a Spitfire and automatically he swept round
on the Messerschmitt's tail and shot the enemy down
before the German knew what was hitting him.

"As the German armoured divisions progressed along
the coast, the fights of Wing Commander Malan and his
Spitfire pilots grew more numerous. From Boulogne to
Dunkirk they patrolled their beat up and down, while the
guns below opened up on them at every opportunity. The
pilots had no respite. The weather on the whole was good

and on no day was it bad enough to give them a breathing spell. On May 24th, by which time Boulogne was in German hands, they came to grips in real earnest with the full weight of the German Luftwaffe. The flight of Spitfires became split up into three sections, one of which was led by Wing Commander Malan who was under severe fire from the German anti-aircraft guns when he got a call over the radio-telephone from his base to say that the Germans were bombing Dunkirk.

"At once he screamed flat out along the coast, dropping down to water level so as to see the enemy against the sky.The sight which met his eyes at Dunkirk was amazing. Never before had he seen anything like it. Formations of twenty to thirty bombers flying at 20,000 feet were grouped together and seemed to stretch in an endless chain as they bombed Dunkirk docks. Above the bombers were countless fighters.

" 'All I saw was the sky black with bombers. I could not see the beginning or end of them,' he reported.

"Climbing all out, he led the other three Spitfires up to the attack. The whole of the German Luftwaffe seemed to be arrayed against them, but they did not falter.

"Straight into one large layer of bombers they sped with guns blazing, cutting deeper and deeper into the formation. The leader gave a Heinkel 111 a burst of five seconds, and as he saw the enemy aircraft take fire he felt a hit by anti-aircraft fire on his starboard wing. At the same moment bullets took a bit out of his flying boot and cut his electric leads.

"Turning steeply starboard, he saw a Messerschmitt 109 firing at him. A glance in his mirror revealed a Messerschmitt 110 firing cannon shell at him from astern. His ring reflector sight with its magic circle of light was put out of action, so his guns were useless without it.

"He was beset with enemies seeking to kill him, threatening to riddle him with their fire. Yet in that crisis he was so cool and calm that he remembered there was a spare ring and bead sight in his locker and he decided to fit it then and there in order to carry on his attack. Climbing steeply into the sun, he pulled the spare sight out of his locker and slipped it into place; but by the time he had accomplished this and turned to take up the attack, the battle had rolled on.

"Looking down, he saw what he thought were three puffs from exploding anti-aircraft shells. A second look disclosed that they were three of the crew of the Heinkel he had destroyed baling out. Those were the first parachutes he had ever seen open in the sky.

"It was such courage displayed by all the British fighter pilots, as well as the pilots and crews of the bombers, which sapped the morale of the German airmen and set the canker of doubt as to their invincibility gnawing in their brains. Wing Commander Malan and his fellow pilots gazed upon the fierce fires which showed how well the British naval units had destroyed Boulogne before giving over to the enemy. Calais succombed after the aircraft of the Royal Air Force had dropped water and food and ammunition into the beleaguered citadel from the air.

"Then the whole might of the Luftwaffe was concentrated on Dunkirk. Every fifteen minutes large masses of German bombers flew over the port and dropped their loads of bombs. At first they kept formation. Then they began to break under the harrying of the Spitfires which seized on the stragglers and shot them down. Seeing their fellows go down in flames also helped to sap the German morale.

"Nightly the Spitfires returned full of bullet holes. Those that could be patched by next day were patched;

the others were discarded and Squadron No. 74 simply raked together all the aircraft it could and plunged at dawn into the struggle once more. They were getting too little sleep, they were working and fighting hard, but the passing of each May day brought with it the knowledge of their growing ascendency over the Germans. They saw the German aircraft begin to waver, then they saw them start to break formation, and in the last days over Dunkirk Wing Commander Malan and the other fighter pilots saw obvious signs of the loss of German morale, for the enemy bomber formations broke up directly they caught sight of the Spitfires and put their noses down and went screaming all out for their own lines and the protection of their anti-aircraft guns.

"When the squadron of Spitfires was taken out of the line for a rest on May 27th, it had definitely destroyed over thirty German aircraft, besides a number that were undoubtedly destroyed, although they were not seen to crash because the pilots were compelled to evade the attacks of the enemy. The squadron's losses were three pilots, of whom one was killed and the other two were taken prisoner.

"Among crowded days later on was one at Dover when Wing Commander Malan led his pilots on four sorties between dawn and 1 o'clock. During that morning they knocked down twenty-four German aircraft and damaged at least eighteen more. Their own losses were four aircraft and two pilots, while two of the pilots baled out safely. By January 1941, Squadron No. 74 under the leadership of Wing Commander Malan had destroyed 127 enemy aircraft, which were seen to crash, while its own losses totalled twelve pilots. The last thirty-three Germans were destroyed without a single loss to themselves.

"That is why the official announcements relax their

usual restraint and refer to his magnificent and brilliant leadership. Before the end of July, 1941, his personal victories totalled at least thirty-five German aircraft which he had shot down and destroyed.

"Lack of decision and incompetence are two of the human failings which the South African cannot tolerate, which probably explains why he has developed such a fine spirit in Squadron No. 74. Fearlessly he led his winged crusaders against the German hordes in the Battle of Britain and every enemy they sent down in flames was another Torch of Freedom lit in the skies to dispel the darkness.

"At the age of thirty, Wing Commander Adolph Gysbert Malan, D.S.O. and Bar, D.F.C. and Bar, has already achieved high honour in the Royal Air Force and added another leaf to the laurels of South Africa."

From *Over To You* by Roald Dahl: "Oh God, how I am frightened. Now that I am alone I don't have to hide it; because there's 21,000 feet between me and them and because now that it's happening again I couldn't pretend any more even if I wanted to. Now I don't have to press my teeth together and tighten the muscles of my jaw as I did during lunch when the corporal brought in the message; when he handed it to Tinker and Tinker looked up at me and said, 'Charlie, it's your turn. You're next up.' As if I didn't know that. As if I didn't know that I was next up. As if I didn't know it last night when I went to bed, and at midnight when I was still awake and all through the night, at one in the morning and at two and three and four and five and six and seven o'clock when I got up. As if I didn't know it when I was dressing and while I was having breakfast and while I was reading the magazines in the mess, playing shove-halfpenny in the mess, reading the notices in the mess, playing billiards in the mess. I knew it then and I knew it when we went in to lunch, while we were eating that mutton for lunch.

"Each time now it gets worse. At first it begins to grow upon you slowly, coming upon you slowly, creeping up on you from behind, making no noise, so that you do not turn round and see it coming. If you saw it coming, perhaps you could stop it, but there is no warning. It creeps closer and closer, like a cat creeps closer stalking a sparrow, and then when it is right behind you, it doesn't spring like the cat would spring; it just leans forward and whispers in your ear. It touches you gently on the shoulder and whispers to you that you are young, that you have a million things to do and a million things to say, that if you are not careful you will buy it, that you are almost certain to buy it sooner or later, and that when you do you will not be anything any longer; you will just be a charred corpse. It whispers to you about how your corpse will look when it is charred, how black it will be and how it will be twisted and brittle, with the face black and fingers black the shoes off the feet because the shoes always come off the feet when you die like that. At first it whispers to you only at night, when you are lying awake in bed at night. Then it whispers to you at odd moments during the day, when you are doing your teeth or drinking a beer or when you are walking down the passage; and in the end it becomes so that you hear it all day and all night all the time.

"The pilot was sitting upright in the cockpit. His face was nearly hidden by his goggles and by his oxygen mask. His right hand was resting lightly upon the stick, and his left hand was forward on the throttle. All the time he was looking around him into the sky. From force of habit his head never ceased to move from one side to the other, slowly, mechanically, like clockwork, so that each moment almost, he searched every part of the blue sky, above, below and all around. But it was into the light of the sun itself that he looked twice as long as he looked anywhere else; for that is the place where the enemy hides and waits before he jumps upon you. There are only two places in which you can hide yourself when you are up in the sky. One is in cloud and the other is in the light of the sun.

"He flew on; and although his mind was working upon many things and although his brain was the brain of a frightened man, yet his instinct was the instinct who is in the sky of the enemy. With a quick glance, without stopping the movement of his head, he looked down and checked his instruments. The glance took no more than a second, and like a camera can record a dozen things at once with the opening of a shutter, so he at a glance recorded with his eyes his oil pressure, his petrol, his oxygen, his rev counter, boost and his air-speed, and in the same instant almost he was looking up again into the sky. He looked at the sun, and as he looked, as he screwed up his eyes and searched into the dazzling brightness of the sun, he thought he saw something. Yes, there it was; a small black speck moving slowly across the bright surface of the sun, and to him the speck was not a speck but a life-size German pilot sitting in a Focke Wulf which had cannon in its wings.

"There was no thought in his head now save for the thought of battle. He was no longer frightened or thinking of being frightened. All that was a dream, and as a sleeper who opens his eyes in the morning and forgets his dream, so this man had seen the enemy and forgotten that he was frightened. It was always the same. It had happened a hundred times before, and now it was happening again. Suddenly, in an instant he had become cool and precise, and as he prepared himself, as he made ready his cockpit, he watched the German, waiting to see what he would do.

"He yanked the stick hard back and over to the left, he kicked hard with the left foot upon the rudder-bar, and like a leaf which is caught up and carried away by a gust of wind, the Spitfire flipped over on its side and changed direction. The pilot blacked out.

"As his sight came back, as the blood drained away from his head and from his eyes, he looked up and saw the German fighter 'way ahead, turning with him, banking hard, trying to turn tighter in order to get back on the tail of the Spitfire. The fight was on. 'Here we go,' he said to himself. 'Here we go again,' and he smiled once, quickly, because he was confident and because he had done this so many time before and because each time he had won."

John C. Mungo-Park: "What I like about Sailor is his quiet, firm manner and his cold courage. He is gifted with such uncanny eyesight and is a 'natural' fighter pilot. When he calls over the R/T 'Let 'em have it! Let 'em have it! there's no messing. The bastards are for it . . ."

BIBLIOGRAPHY
Bekker, Cajus, *The Luftwaffe War Diaries*, Doubleday, 1968
Bishop, Edward, *The Battle of Britain*, Allen and Unwin, 1960
Bungay, Stephen, *The Most Dangerous Enemy*, Aurum, 2009
Collier, Richard, *Eagle Day*, Pan Books, 1968
Deere, Alan, *Nine Lives*, Hodder & Stoughton, 1959
Deighton, Len, *Fighter*, Ballantine Books, 1977
Duke, Neville, *Test Pilot*, Grub Street, 2003
Forrester, Larry, *Fly For Your Life*, Bantam, 1978
Galland, Adolf, *The First and the Last*, Ballantine Books, 1954
Glancey, Jonathan, *Spitfire The Biography*, Atlantic Books, 2006
Hall, Roger, *Clouds of Fear*, Coronet Books, 1975
Hillary, Richard, *The Last Enemy*, Macmillan, 1950
Johnson, J.E., *Wing Leader*, Ballantine Books, 1957
Mason, F. K., *Battle Over Britain*, Alban Books
Masters, David, *So Few*, Eyre & Spottiswoode, 1942
Murrow, Edward R., *This Is London*, Simon & Schuster, 1941
Orde, Cuthbert, *Pilots of Fighter Command*, G. G. Harrap, 1942
Page, Geoffrey, *Tale of a Guinea Pig*, Wingham Press, 1991
Quill, Geoffrey, *Spitfire*, Arrow Books, 1985
Tidy, Douglas, *I Fear No Man*, Macdonald, 1972
Townsend, Peter, *Duel of Eagles*, Simon & Schuster, 1970
Walker, Oliver, *Sailor Malan*, Cassell, 1953
Wood, D. and Dempster, D., *The Narrow Margin*, McGraw-HillAberdeen, 167

Adam, Ronald, 89
Adler Tag, 76
Angels One Five, 158
Anglo-American Corp., 194
Antrim, Lord, 41
Ayers, D.H., 143
Aubert, Bertie, 134, 135
Bader, Douglas, 99, 104, 162, 166
Barking Creek, Battle of, 72, 73
Barrow-in-Furness, 167
Bartley, Tony, 141, 190
Battle of Britain film, 148, 156, 157, 158
Beaufighter, Bristol, 101
Beaufort Club, 128, 129
Beauvoir, Simone de, 29
Beaverbrook, Lord, 150
Benfontein, 196
Bentley Priory, 72, 190
Bf 109, Messerschmitt, 62, 63, 65, 74, 82
Bf 110, Messerschmitt, 124, 140, 166
Biggin Hill, 51, 52, 70, 79, 88, 100, 103, 110, 111, 113, 121-130, 139, 140, 142, 150, 186,

187
Bigglesworth, James, 150
Birkenhead, 167
Birmingham, 61, 167
Blenheim, 142
Boelcke, Oswald, 98, 99
Botha Boys, 21
Botha, Louis, 20, 204
Boulding, R.J.E., 143, 186
Boulogne, 103
Bourne, David, 174
Boy's High School, 15
Brasted, 190
Brighton, 167
Bristol Aeroplane Co. Flying School, 38
Bristol and Colonial Aeroplane Co., 38
Bristol Filton Flying Ground, 38
Bristol, 167
British Apprentice Club, 29, 30
Britain, Battle of, 48, 51, 57, 59, 60, 63, 65, 66, 70, 73, 75, 76, 79, 82, 88, 90, 99, 104, 110, 111, 122, 125, 126, 129, 143, 148, 149, 151, 156, 160, 162, 163, 166, 173, 182, 183, 204, 205
Brookes, D.S., 191
Brzezina, Stanislaw, 79, 143
Bungay, Stephen, 189
Burnard, F.P., 143
Byrne, Vincent, 72
Caine, Michael, 157
Calais, 73, 74
Canberra, English Electric, 40
Canewdon, 74
Cape Town, 201
Cardiff, 167
Castle Bromwich, 61
Chamberlain, Neville, 56
Charrett, Arthur, 50
Chartwell, 80, 125
Chelsea, Hotel, 29
Chesters, P., 143
Churchill, Winston, 76, 80, 89, 125, 150, 160
Churches, E.W.G., 143
Clacton, 124
Clarke, Arthur C., 29
Clydebank, 167
Coltishall, 79, 166
Conway, HMS, 21
Condor Legion, 63, 96, 125
Coolidge, Calvin, 28
Crossley, Michael, 122, 190
Croydon, 122, 123

Aberdeen, 132
Adam, Ronald, 71
Adler Tag, 60
Anderson shelter, 136
Angels One Five, 125
Anglo-American Corp.,
155
Antrim, Lord, 34
Apartheid, 156
Armstrong, W., 115
Aubert, Berty, 106, 107
Audax, Hawker, 31
Ayers, D.H., 115
Bader, Douglas, 79,
129, 131
Barrow-in-Furness, 132
Bartley, Tony, 113, 153
Battle of Barking Creek,
56, 57
Battle of Britain, 7, 38,
41, 46, 47, 50, 52, 54,
57, 59, 60, 62, 63, 70,
72, 79, 84, 87, 100,
104, 117, 118, 123,
126, 127, 130, 131,
138, 146, 154, 156,
159, 165, 166, 175
Battle of Britain, 117,
123, 125, 130
Battle of France, 47
Battle of Jutland, 28, 45
Battle of the Somme, 38
Beamish, Victor, 167
Beaufighter, Bristol, 81
Beaufort Club, 103, 104
Beaverbrook, Lord, 119
Belfast, 132
Belfast *Daily Telegraph*,
34
Benfontein, 157
Bentley Priory, 56
Berlin Olympics, 50
Bf 109, Messerschmitt,
49, 50, 52, 58, 59, 61,
64, 74, 78, 80, 81, 82,
83, 89, 102, 103, 106,
107, 109, 111, 114,
131, 149
Bf 110, Messerschmitt,
99, 112, 113, 131, 180
Biggin Hill, 41, 42, 63,

64, 80, 83, 87, 88, 90,
97, 98, 99, 100, 101,
102, 103, 104, 111,
112, 114, 119, 121,
149, 150, 151, 153,
167, 169, 170, 172, 173
Bigglesworth ,James,
120
Birkinhead, 132
Birmingham, 132
Blackburn, 45
Blenheim, Bristol, 114
Boelcke, Oswald, 78, 79
Boer, 11, 12, 13
Boston, Douglas, 171
Botha boys, 17, 19
Botha, Louis, 16, 165
Bouchier, C.A., 167,
168, 169
Boulding, R.J.E., 115,
149, 150
Boulogne, 83, 179, 181
Bourne, David, 139
Brighton, 132
Bristol, 45, 132
Bristol Aeroplane Co.
Flying School, 30, 31
Bristol Filton Flying
Ground, 30
British Apprentice
Club, 23, 24
Brookes, D.S., 153
Brzezina, Stanislaw, 63,
115
Burnard, F.P., 115
Bungay, Stephen, 152
Byrne, Vincent, 56
Caine, Michael, 124
Cape Town, 9, 15, 117,
158, 162
Cap Gris Nez, 62
Castle Bromwich, 48
Cardiff, 132
Chamberlain, Neville,
43
Charles, Jack, 170
Charrett, Arthur, 40
Chartwell, 64
Chesters, P., 115
Churches, E.W.G, 115
Churchill, Winston, 7,

43, 60, 64, 71, 100,
119, 128
Clarke, Arthur C., 23
Clydebank, 132
Coltishall, 63, 131
Condor Legion, 50, 76,
100
Conway, HMS, 17
Coolidge, Calvin, 22
Courtrai, 170
Coventry, 132
Crossley, Michael, 97,
153
Croydon, 98
Curtiss airfield, 173
Daimler Benz, 49, 50
Dahl, Roald, 183
Davis, Elmer, 141
Davis, Howard, 16
Davis, T.B.F., 16
Deere, Al, 36, 37, 38,
39, 41, 42, 54, 57, 84,
96, 119, 129, 167
Deighton, Len, 149
De Beauvoir, Simone, 24
De Kooning, Willem, 23
De Wilde, 96
Dempster, Derek, 138
Dickson, Lovat, 87
Do 17, Dornier, 60, 100
Do 215, Dornier, 98,
108
Dover, 61, 62, 65, 70,
99, 108, 111, 182
Dowding, D.H.T., 115
Dowding, H.C.T., 37,
46, 47, 57, 100, 124,
127, 129, 145, 153
Draper, B.V., 112, 113,
115
Duke, Neville, 87, 88,
89, 90, 101
Duke-Wooley, R.M.B.,
150
Dungeness, 114
Dunkirk, 57, 58, 96,
106, 179, 180, 181
Durban, 16
Duxford, 111, 125
Eagle Squadron, 125
Eastbourne, 132

Eastleigh, 43, 46
Eighth Air Force, U.S., 53, 79, 129
85 Squadron, 68
Eley, F.W., 115
Exeter, 132
False Bay, 15
54 Squadron, 40, 54
56 Squadron, 55, 56, 57
Fighter Squadron, 125
First of the Few, 125
Flavell, Geoffrey, 145
Flying Tigers, 125
Fw 190, Focke-Wulf, 168, 169, 170, 171, 185
Fokker E.1, 78
403 Squadron, 168
Francis, C.W., 115
Franklin, W.D.K., 115
Fraser, Lynda, 27, 32, 43, 147, 155
Freeborn, John, 56, 57, 106, 108, 115, 131, 178, 179
Freese, L.E., 115
Galland, Adolf, 130
Gauntlet, Gloster, 33, 35, 41
General Botha, 14, 16, 17, 20, 21, 22, 28
Gibson, Wilfred, 143
Gillan, John, 34
Gladiator, Gloster, 45
Glancey, Jonathan. 51
Glasgow, 132
Gleave, Tom, 129
Glendinning, J.N. 115
Gloster, 45
Gobden, D.G., 115
Goering, Hermann, 128, 131
Golden Valley Citrus Estates, 21
Gravelines, 82, 113
Gray, Colin, 54, 153
Grice, Richard, 98
Grosvenor House, 103
Gunn, H.R., 108, 109, 115
Hamilton, Guy, 123
Hart, Hawker, 39

Hastings, D., 115
Hawkinge, 70, 109, 125
Heinkel 111, 58, 59, 112, 131, 147, 148, 177, 180
Heinkel 113, 111
Hell's Corner, 62
Henshaw, Alexl 48
Hendrix, Jimi, 23
Hepburn, Katharine, 45
Highveld, 11
Hilken, C.G., 115
Hillary, Richard, 87, 101
Hind, Hawker, 31
Hitler, Adolf, 43, 52, 66, 128, 131, 132, 156
Hoad, Norman, 153
Hood, HMS, 15
Hornchurch, 34, 35, 40, 54, 69, 70, 71, 148, 167
Hotel Chelsea, 23
Howard, J., 115
Howard, Trevor, 124
Huguenot College, 9
Hulton-Harrop, M., 56, 57
Hurricane, Hawker, 44, 46, 52, 55, 56, 64, 72, 97, 98, 108, 125, 128, 141
Immelman, Max, 79
Johns, Jasper, 23
Johns, W.E., 120
Jones, Ira, 69
Joplin, Janis, 23
Johnson, Johnnie, 151, 170
Junkers, 49
Ju 88, Junkers, 58, 111, 177, 178
Jürgens, Kurt, 124
Kelly, Piers, 59, 60, 108, 109, 115
Kennedy, Joseph P., 135
Kenley, 70, 82, 98, 150, 169, 170
Kent, Johnny, 129, 153
Kimberley, 153, 157, 165
King George VI, 119

King Louis XIV, 9
Kingcome, Brian, 153
Kingston-upon-Hull, 132
Kirk, T.P., 113, 115
Kirton-in-Lindsay, 63, 74
Kromme River, 9
K5054, 53
Lacey, James, 129, 130
Langtry, Lillie, 24
Le Bourget, 22
Le Touquet, 168
Leigh-Mallory, Trafford, 81, 82
Lindemann, Frederick, 100
Lindbergh, Charles, 22, 23, 173
Liverpool, 132
Lucking, D.F., 55, 56
Lusser, Robert, 49
Mahaddie, Hamish, 129
Maidstone, 97, 112
Malan, Daniel, 13, 117,
Malan, Evelyn, 10
Malan, Jonathan, 147
Malan, Piet, 11
Malan, Ralph, 12, 15
Malan, Willem, 10, 11, 14
Malaya, HMS, 28
Manchester, 132
Mandela, Nelson, 118
Mannock, Mick, 67, 68, 151
Manston, 59, 62, 65, 70, 99, 108, 110, 113, 114, 149
Martell, Chris, 170
Martlesham, 70
Masters, David, 151, 176
Mayne, E., 115
Mayo, Katherine, 24
McClean, Robert, 45
McShane, Ian, 124
Measures, W.E.G., 115
Messerschmitt, Willy, 49
Midway, 125
Mikhoog, 14

Miller, Arthur, 23
Milne, Dicky, 167, 168, 170
Mitchell, Alan, 171
Mitchell, Douglas, 163
Mitchell, Reginald, 44, 46
Mölders, Werner, 59, 76, 77, 78
More, Kenneth, 124
Morrison shelter, 136
Morrison, N., 115
Mosely, Leonard, 123
Mortimer, Joan, 98, 99
Mould, Tony, 106, 108, 115
Mungo-Park, J.C., 54, 64, 65, 101, 106, 107, 112, 115, 186
Murrow, Edward R., 140
Mussolini, Benito, 43
Nasson, Bill, 117, 118, 119, 120
Nelson, W.H., 115
Newell, Moyca, 24
Ninth Air Force, U.S., 79
19 Squadron, 111
92 Squadron, 100
North Weald, 55, 57, 123, 125, 126
Nottingham, 132
Observer Corps., 47, 58
151 Squadron, 55
O'Neill, Eugene, 23
Olivier, Laurence, 124, 129
Oppenheimer, Ernest, 155
Oppenheimer, Harry, 155, 156, 157, 159, 161
Oppenheimer, Robert, 24
Operation Sea Lion, 52, 70, 128
Orde, Cuthbert, 146, 153, 174, 175
Orange Free State, 11
Orteig, Raymond, 22
Oxspring, Bobby, 101
Paardeberg, 10

Page, Geoffrey, 153
Pangbourne, HMS, 17
Park, Keith, 60, 70, 81, 124
Parkes, Sgt., 115
Pas de Calais, 82
Pearl Harbor, 125
Peace, P/O, 115
Phone War, 47
Piaf, Edith, 24
Pipsqueak, 63
Plummer, Christopher, 125
Plymouth, 132
Portsmouth, 132
Preston, Kath, 101
Prince of Wales, 20
Pyle, Ernie, 132
Queen Elizabeth, HMS, 28
Queen Mary, 43
Quill, Jeffrey, 45, 48, 110
Rand War Veterans Action Committee, 118, 158
Rankin, Jamie, 88, 114, 153
Reach For The Sky, 125
R.D.F. chain, 57, 58, 70, 127
Reichsluftfahrtministerium, 49
Repulse, HMS, 20
Reynolds, Quentin, 139, 175
Richardson, Ralph, 124
Richthofen, Manfred von, 79, 80, 151
Riebeck Kasteel, 117
Riverside, 27
Rochford, 107
Rolls-Royce, 51, 53
Rolls-Royce Merlin, 50
Rose, Frank, 57
Roosevelt Field, 22
Roosevelt, Franklin, 135
Sandown Castle, 22, 28
Sartre, Jean-Paul, 24
Sassoon Cup, 41

Scala gun battery, 21
Scott, J..A., 115
74 Squadron, 41, 43, 54, 55, 58, 60, 62, 63, 65, 66, 67, 70, 74, 80, 88, 99, 100, 108, 111, 112, 117, 131, 149, 154, 176, 183
Shakespeare, William, 43
Shaw, Robert, 117, 123, 124
Sheffield, 132
Shilling, Beatrice, 51
Sholto Douglas, William, 81, 82
Simonstown, 15, 21
6 Flying Training School, 38, 39
65 Squadron, 41, 54
66 Squadron, 100, 112
609 Squadron, 88
610 Squadron, 97, 98
611 Squadron, 167
Skinner, W.M., 107, 116, 148
Slent, 10, 12, 14
Slessor, J.C., 174
Smith, A.J., 116
Smith, D.N.E., 116
Smuts, Jan Christiaan, 11, 155, 165
Southampton, 132
Spanish Civil War, 44, 50, 76, 100
Spaulding, Mrs H.C., 174
Spitfire, HMS, 45
Spirit of St. Louis, 22, 173
Springbok Legion, 118
Spurdle, R.L., 113, 116
St. John, P.C.B., 108, 115
St. Omer, 113, 168
St. Paul's, 134
Stalag Luft III, 32
Stellenbosch, 13, 14
Stephen, H.M., 54, 108, 112, 116, 145, 152
Stirling, Short, 129

Summers, Mutt, 46
Supermarine, 46
Sutton Bridge, 74
Swansea, 132
Szczesny, Henryk, 63, 64, 116
Tangmere, 70
Thames, HMS, 16, 21
Thames estuary, 60
32 Squadron, 97
Thomas, Dylan, 23
3 Flying Training School, 30, 31, 32
Tiger Moth, De Havilland, 30
Torch Commando, 118, 155-166
Transvaal, 11, 13
Treacy, Paddy, 33, 43, 106, 107
Trenchard, Hugh, 31
Tuck, R.R.Stanford, 32 33, 54, 101, 129, 130, 153
Tunbridge Wells, 98
Twain, Mark, 23
Twenty-four Rivers, 11
Uxbridge, 32, 81, 97, 125
Val du Charron, 9
Vickers-Supermarine Spitfire, 32, 36, 41, 43-53, 54, 55, 56, 58, 59, 61, 63, 70, 72, 74, 83, 86, 98, 100, 102, 106, 108, 109, 110, 112, 122, 124, 126, 128, 141, 147, 148, 168, 178, 179, 181, 182, 186
Victory, HMS, 17
Walker, Oliver, 16, 84, 143, 164, 165, 173
Warhol, Andy, 24
Wellington, 9, 10, 14, 15, 117
White, F.L., 116
White Hart, 152
Whitstable, 100
Williams, Tennessee, 23
Winant, John, 135, 136\
Wittering, 63

Wolfe, Thomas, 23
Wood, Derek, 138
Worcester, HMS, 16, 17
York, Susannah, 125
Young, J.H.R., 108, 116